THE LUCY MEMORIAL FREED SLAVES' HOME

*The Sudan United Mission and
The British Colonial Government in Partnership*

Virginia A. Salamone
Frank A. Salamone

University Press of America,® Inc.
Lanham · Boulder · New York · Toronto · Plymouth, UK

Copyright © 2008 by
University Press of America,® Inc.
4501 Forbes Boulevard
Suite 200
Lanham, Maryland 20706
UPA Acquisitions Department (301) 459-3366

Estover Road
Plymouth PL6 7PY
United Kingdom

Library of Congress Control Number: 2007933323
ISBN-13: 978-0-7618-3891-3 (paperback : alk. paper)
ISBN-10: 0-7618-3891-0 (paperback : alk. paper)

Cover photos top to bottom:
Northfield Seminary in Massachusetts;
Northfield Seminary, another view, where Lucy Died;
Gravestone: "Mam-ma's Grave";
Gravestone: "Love Never Faileth"

⊖™ The paper used in this publication meets the minimum
requirements of American National Standard for Information
Sciences—Permanence of Paper for Printed Library Materials,
ANSI Z39.48—1984

Dedication

We dedicate this book to our children, parents, and friends.
We also dedicate it to the spirit of a courageous woman,
Lucy Guinness Kumm, who was ahead of her time.
Her mighty efforts led to a significant organization,
whose work continues to this day.

We also dedicate this book to the memory of Ibrahim,
who was a student and friend,
murdered in the prime of his productive and loving life.

Contents

Preface

This is a labor of love. In 1977 shortly after we were married, we went to Nigeria to teach at the University of Jos. Virginia was teaching education courses and Frank Anthropology and African Studies. We soon discovered that we had a good deal of free time since the school year was out of synch with the true date because of various strikes and other difficulties. So we began to conduct research in the archives in Kaduna. While there, Virginia began to read about the Lucy Memorial Freed Slaves' Home.

After leaving Nigeria, we spent some time reading in the British Library over the years, making copies of government reports. Frank began to follow the archives to various parts of England, wherever the Sudan United Mission (SUM), later the Action Group, moved them. The archives began in a chaotic state, kept in old traveling trunks. Eventually, the Action Group had them put on microfilm and there is a plan to digitalize them and make them available through computers. We have checked the microfilm copies and find we have them in our photocopied records.

The time came to write the brief history of the Home. We decided to keep it simple and short. There is some material placing the Home in a wider historical and theoretical setting. We also provide a brief history of the SUM. However, we wish to keep the focus on Lucy, the SUM, and the Home. We share with Lucy an abhorrence of slavery wherever and whenever practiced. We do not share a hatred of Islam nor a belief that British colonialism was a good thing. We do try to be objective, however, in looking at expatriate society in Nigeria in the early 20th Century.

This book has been a long time in coming. We hope others will be fascinated by Lucy's story and the work at the Home. We met people in Nigeria who were descendants of people from the Home or who knew those who had been there. These were decent people, living productive lives. We will never forget them and their unfailing kindness to us.

Virginia and Frank Salamone
White Plains, NY
April 15, 2007

Acknowledgments

We acknowledge the unfailing help of the Action Group with this research. They gave us carte blanche in using their material. The provided work space, meals, and free copying, with no restrictions. Their behavior was a testimony to their faith. We also wish to thank the Nigerian National Archives and British Library for their help.

Chapter One

Lucy Guinness Kumm

The Lucy Memorial Freed Slaves' Home operated in Nigeria from 1909 until 1925 as a memorial to the memory of Lucy Guinness Kumm. During its 16 years, the Home provided care, education, job training, and emotional support for hundreds of emancipated slaves. Examination of Lucy Guinness Kumm's life offers, in addition to another inspirational example of the complete dedication many woman missionaries had to their vocation, a demonstration of the impact one woman's work could have upon the vocational decisions and expression of social activism of others. Lucy, as one of three founders of the Sudan United Mission, came to serve as a role model for subsequent woman missionaries and supporters.

Lucy Evangeline Guinness was born in Great Britain in July, 1865. Both sides of her family held a history of foreign military and evangelical service. Her father, Henry Grattan Guinness had been ordained into the ministry in 1857 and had pledged himself to evangelical work. Her mother, Fanny Fitzgerald Guinness, was a prolific writer applying her talents toward mission publication and working with her husband on his evangelical efforts. During her youth, Lucy's parents founded the East London Institute dedicated to missionary training and publication of mission material. A major source for material on Lucy's life comes from a biography written by her father. By her parents standards, her birth into a family of active missionaries was not reference or qualification enough for fitness for God's work but they had aspirations for her worthiness being shown to them. In her biography her father writes,

(W)e called her Lucy—from lux, lumiere, light—hoping that God would make her a light to those in darkness; and Evangeline, angel, or messenger of good tidings, desiring that such she might become. (Guinness 1907: 6-7)

Her parents kept watch over Lucy and her siblings for incidents and behaviors indicative of her fitness. Her father recalls an incident from her childhood that he interpreted as God's acceptance of Lucy's evangelical fitness. The evidence came to him at a time when. Lucy was gravely ill. Guinness writes, ". . . well do I remember the agony of prayer on her behalf that she might be spared, and raised up to become a useful servant of the Lord. Those prayers were richly answered" (Guinness 1907:7-8).

Lucy's subsequent enthusiastic participation in religious activities offered her by her parents further convinced them that Lucy's heart was won by their Savior, and they continually encouraged her participation in religious activities. Lucy traveled extensively with her family. Daring her travels she focused upon the living conditions and the quality-of-life of the indigenous people. At 17 she accompanied her brother, who was involved in his own training as a missionary, on a 2 1/2 year trip to Australia and Tasmania. During her vacations from school in Melbourne, Lucy accompanied her brother on his field trips, gathering information on local life and customs. Upon her return to Great Brittan she lived with her parents at the East London Institute, an area of London her father described as ". . . in a neighborhood whose only attraction was the sphere it afforded for evangelistic and philanthropic work" (Guinness 1907:9). At this time Lucy's concern for others expressed itself in social activism. She began researching and writing on contemporary issues for publication.

Only a Factory Girl was probably Lucy's first publication. Published in 1886 when she was 21, *Only a Factory Girl* is a sympathetic account of a day in the night of an East London factory girl. Posing undercover, dressed as a factory girl Lucy, accompanied by a family maid, lived and worked in the West London factory district. The excerpts following illustrate Lucy's literary style that strove to move her readers from their armchair in a comfortable, secure home, into an uncomfortable, insecure, fragile life, and then back again to their armchair, motivated by righteous indignation to act upon one or more courses of action suggested by the author and the subjects of her research. Henry Grattan

Guinness's biography of his daughter's life includes an extensive section of extracts of her writings. His extracts begin with Lucy's description of the factory area, move through her description of the activities available to the girls during their non-working hours and conclude with her suggestions for bettering the quality-of-life. His extracts do not indicate where omissions of the original text are made.

> It is nearly midnight. A damp, drizzling rain, falling chillily, is making the black mud of the pavements blacker and more slippery than ever. Surely there are no factory girls about the streets at this hour! The narrow streets are full of refuse of every description. The theatres have just shut up, turning their occupants on to the streets—or, rather, into the public-houses. We went "into the warm" and had not to look far to discover the objects of our search. Numbers of these young factory girls were there, some of them with quite pretty faces, half stupid with drink, and wholly unable to take care of themselves, hearing the vilest language, and surrounded by degrading and shameful sights. We have often wondered at the language and uncontrollable wildness of factory girls. After to-night's experience, we shall never wonder again, but rather marvel that, seeing their lives are such, and that such places are open to them nightly, they should ever be content to come to our evening classes and sit and sew and spell! (Guinness 1907:58-59)

Lucy writes that not all of the factory girls frequent the public houses and she and her companion seek them out. Of those girls she writes:

> No one cares that we stand wet through and cold, with the chill rain beating on our bare hands and shabby clothing, at the entrance of an evil looking lane. Our companions are standing here too other girls dressed as we are: unwilling as we are—though for very different reasons—to go home. Oh, friends, let us speak to you as if we were one with these girls! We will put ourselves in their place and be factory girls for the time. (Guinness 1907:61)

Along the road from her own feeling of indignation toward a suitable remedy, Lucy enlisted the support of a cross-section of the literate population including political, social, and religious leaders and the day worker and family. As a result of her undercover research and publication, a home for factory girls was established by and under the care of the daughter of a university professor from Aberdeen.

The growing missions of the late 1800's offered Lucy a continually growing audience. Her thoughts and suggested solutions were published in a variety of forms. Articles, books, mission reports, poetry, and pamphlets designed to provide an overview of one issue were used to inform, involve, encourage, motivate, and resolve. She sought to reach a literate audience through a variety of literary styles. Her writing range included sentimental poetry and ethnographic and statistical information.

After the publication of *Only a Factory Girl* and publications written in a similar social activist style, Lucy's writing began to take on a religious perspective. Her father credits this change in perspective to "(H)er residence with us at Barley House (East London Institute) brought Lucy much into contact with missionaries and mission work, and so awakened her interest in the evangelization of the world . . ." (Guinness 1907: 9). Enriching the quality-of-life was Lucy's focus, and evangelization and education were to become her methods.

Lucy wrote and spoke extensively on the geopolitical areas open to Christian evangelical efforts. After her mother's death, she assumed the editorship of the mission publication, *Regions and Beyond*. Much of her writing was done as editor and not credited to her directly. Quite probably works credited to other authors contain thoughts first developed by Lucy. A note in Bore (1979) observes "one is struck by the similarity of such passages from Kumm's hand to those written by his first wife. The sentiments he wrote with respect to Africa, she put down about Latin America" (Bore 1979:131). In addition to her more than 10 years as the *Regions and Beyond* editor, Lucy researched and published on topics that included opium addiction in the Orient and its impact upon the economy of Great Britain and the evangelical potential of South America and India.

Of her writing ability her father wrote,

> she possessed a genius for the use of appropriate language, a discriminating touch on the rich instrument of speech which qualifies her to be the writer she became. To make her subject live, to put into words the soul of her meaning, came naturally to her. She did not aim at eloquence, or affect the perfection of a classical style, but wrote clearly and simply, with fullness, feeling, and power. (Guinness 1907:6-7)

Assessing Lucy's writings with hindsight exposes some flaws in her methods of gathering demographic material, flaws that would not have been discernable to her contemporaries. Contemporary literary criticisms offered Lucy's works high praise and recommendation. Reviews and advertisements for her publications include phrases such as: "Deeply interesting—a very attractive volume; (I)t will touch chords of loving sympathy all over the world; (T)his lovely tribute . . . will delight every reader. No one should miss this fascinating and inspiring missionary romance" (Guinness 1907: endpapers).

Lucy was also assessed a competent and inspiring public speaker. Her biography includes several references to her desire to and delight in addressing both large and intimate gatherings. In an attempt to expand British support for the Sudan United Mission, her father notes,

> Lucy made bold to visit in person a number of the most influential Christian ministers in the land, and formed English, Scotch, and Irish councils of the Mission, in London, Edinburg, and Dublin, numbering among their members 5 and 20 leading men in the various denominations. (Guinness 1907:20)

Several examples of her zeal and impact upon large audiences are noted in her biography both through her father's observations and through letters sent him, in praise of his daughter, by those who had heard Lucy speak for the mission. Lucy had a close personal and working relationship with her father. In 1900 both extended their personal and working relationship to include Lucy's husband, H. Karl Wilhelm Kumm.

Lucy's mother died in 1899. Soon after her death, Lucy and her father traveled to Egypt and the Holy Land. The trip, in part, was to serve to help them recover from the emotional stress both had felt at her passing. Several times during their trip, they passed through Egypt where Kumm, a young German missionary, was working on completion of a Bishareen vocabulary which he planned to use in his evangelical activities. During their encounters Lucy and Karl found they shared an immediate interest in the lives of the people of Egypt and the long-ranged goal for linking the Niger and Nile Rivers with a chain of mission stations. The sharing of these goals drew the couple closer.

On January 11, 1900 Lucy and Karl received Guinnesses's consent to marry. Her father writes "(A)s a token of this consent their hands were joined above the clasped hands of two Bishareen" (Guinness 1907:18). This inclusion of those whose lives Lucy and Karl would dedicate themselves to try to enhance at this intimate moment was indicative of the commitment, dedication, and personal regard with which the couple held their potential missioners. Lucy and Karl were married in Cairo on February 3, 1900. Lucy was 35 and Karl 25. Kumm's linguistic entries to Bishareen culture, joined by Guinness's organization and evangelical talents and Lucy's particular literary talents led to the creation of a small mission outpost which was to evolve into the Sudan United Mission.

For the next 6 years until her death in Northfield, Massachusetts, H. Grattan, Lucy, and Karl planned mission philosophy, strategy, and action. Lucy's biography and her husband's writings indicate she served as a model for the role Guinness and Kumm would present as appropriate and desirable for woman in the SUM. Evidence of this comes from the First Annual Report of the South African Branch of the SUM published in 1908.

In addition, at Dr. Kumm's suggestion, a very effective Ladies' Committee was formed, the object of which was threefold.

1. Prayer for the Mission work in the Sudan
2. Spreading news about this work and getting others interested in the work.
3. Collecting subscriptions from South Africans for the support of Missionaries.

The effectiveness of the Ladies' Committee at meeting these objectives can be found in subsequent annual reports. These reports included annual reports of the Ladies' Central Committee Lightbearer's League and outlined the committees' activities including: continual growth in membership each year, the acceptance of woman from their region into fieldwork, steady growth in contributions of money and services, and a successful drive to include schoolchildren in a foster parent type subscription program in support of freed slave children taken into the Lucy Memorial Home.

Lucy Kumm's influence and impact on the activities and ideals of the Sudan United Mission is evidenced by these excerpts from a booklet entitled *The Lucy Memorial Freed Slave's Home*.

The formation of the Sudan United Mission will ever be associated with the burning missionary zeal and consecrated life of the late Mrs. Karl Kumm, the last years of whose life were devoted to the organization of an effort to carry the Gospel to the Sudan. . . .(3) After careful and prayerful consideration it was unanimously decided to found a Freed Slaves' Home as a lasting memorial to her life and work.(4)

In The *Open Sore of Africa: Slave Raiding* Lucy's husband writes:

(W)hat more fitting memorial to the life of the late Mrs. Kumm could be devised than a home for those rescued from the awful fate of slavery—a home where Christian love would reign, and the gospel of redeeming grace be taught, a home where lives shall be delivered from sin and suffering and be transformed into sanctified, consecrated service to Christ.(15-16)

Her obituary reads,

Mrs. Karl Kumm passed away suddenly at Northfield, Mass., early on the morning of August 12. Mrs. Kumm was the younger daughter of Dr. Grattan Guinness of Harly House, London, founder of the "Regions Beyond Missionary Union." Before her marriage with Dr. Kumm, a missionary to the Soudan, she was for some years editor of the Regions Beyond, the organ of the R.B.M.U. As Lucy Guinness, too, she published a brochure on India and also edited a collection of letters written by her sister, Mrs. Howard Taylor, one of the China Island Missionaries, entitled *In the Far East.* At the time of her death, Mrs. Kumm had just finished an expose of the Congo atrocities, in the reform of which she took a more than keen interest. This book will shortly be published under the title of *Our Slave State: An Appeal to the Nations.*

Beside her husband, who at the time of her death was unfortunately in England, Mrs. Kumm leaves two little sons. (Obituary. Record of Christian Work. Vol. 25, No. 9, 1906 Copyright Sept. 1906. W. R. Moody, p. 763).

Chapter Two

The Founding of the Sudan United Mission

The Sudan United Mission was a union of a number of different evangelical missions, dedicated to evangelizing areas of Africa which were under "threat" by Muslim proselytizers. Originally termed the Sudan Pioneer Mission, and currently known as Action Partners, the organization was founded in 1904 by Dr. Hermann Karl Wilhelm Kumm (1875-1930), from Osterode, Germany, his wife Lucy Evangeline Guinness (1865-1906), and her father Henry Grattan Guinness (1835-1910), a fiery evangelist and founder of the East London Institute.

The term Sudan referred to more than simply the country of that name. To Karl Kumm it meant the Greater Sudan, an area stretching from Nigeria to Chad and the Anglo-Egyptian Sudan in the east. The goal of the SUM was to stop the spread of Islam. In July 1904 the SUM sent its first four missionaries to the Benue River area of Nigeria. These four men had the task of starting a church in the area, using evangelism, education, and medical work.

The first four SUM missionaries included Karl Kumm, J. Lowry Maxwell, John G. Burt, and Ambrose H. Bateman. These four men sailed on the "Akabo" for Nigeria on July 23, 1904. Upon arrival they worked their way in from the coast. The High Commissioner, Sir Frederick Lugard, recommended that they go to the Benue area of Nigeria and work in the hill area near the town of Wase. Wase was about eighty miles from the Benue River. En route Bateman had to return to England with appendicitis. Maxwell and Burt continued south of the Benue to Wukari, another twenty-three miles south and established a mission among the Jukun people. Karl Kumm stated the case clearly,

The whole raison d'être of the . . . Mission is to counteract the Moslem advance among the Pagan tribes in the Benue region. This cannot be done by going to the Mohammedans and therefore our work will lie among the Pagan tribes. . . . Even while I was still in England a voice seemed to say to me, "I have prepared the people of the desert for my Gospel, go and preach it to them." Now at last I have had a look upon those dear people and upon the vast desert Sahara, which is for me the Promised Land. Yet it was only a short look and I had to come away again to abide the Lord's time. . . .

Kumm's wife, Lucy Guinness, proved a great inspiration to him and was a great help in establishing the SUM. She had quite a career before marrying him, aiding her father in his work and doing what today would be termed investigative journalism. She had gone undercover as a factory worker in the East End, exposing the mistreatment of young female workers. She edited the *Regions Beyond Missionary Union Magazine*, and toured African mission stations, gathering first-hand knowledge and experience of the Greater Sudan. Eventually she met and married Karl Kumm in Cairo.

She agreed with Kumm on the importance of evangelizing the Sudan. Over fifty million people lived in the Greater Sudan in the late 19th Century. Islam was fast spreading over the region and no Free Church of Great Britain had a mission station in the region. Thus they formed the German Sudan Pioneer Mission in 1900. Upon returning to England they soon severed ties with the German group and formed the Sudan Pioneer Mission in 1902, meeting in Sheffield. However, the mission was not large enough for them and they held a meeting in Edinburgh, Scotland, on June 15, 1904, forming the Sudan United Mission. The new mission was open to people of all denominations. The SUM was interested in people who were committed to converting the population of the Greater Sudan and stopping the spread of Islam. Almost immediately, Maxwell, Bateman, and Burt came forward.

Kumm was an indefatigable recruiter, hoping to recruit 150 missionaries for 50 stations. He envisioned stations where traditional religions and Islam met. In his words, "at least three white missionaries, a medical man, an ordained educationalist and a horticulturalist" would be stationed at each mission. He toured Britain in 1905 seeking missionaries. Then he went to Australia, New Zealand, Tasmania, South Africa, Denmark, Canada, and the United States, seeking money and missionaries for his non-denominational missionary movement. Initially, the missionaries worked without regard for their place of origin. After a time, missionaries from different nations set up their missions in different regions, leading to different churches. The British branch of the SUM became the Church of Christ in Nigeria (COCIN). The work of this branch was centered in the Benue River area of Nigeria.

The mission work progressed well, expanding from the Jukun to other groups. At Rumasha the SUM baptized their first African convert, a young man fabled in their tales, Tom Aliyana, who had worked first for the Church Mission Society. The SUM, in fact, had spread across the Greater Sudan and had stations in the Anglo-Egyptian Sudan itself. It had stations in Nigeria, French Cameroon, and French Equatorial Africa as well. By the mid-1930s there were 130 European missionaries, close to the 150 Kumm had originally wanted.

One of the reasons for the establishment of the SUM was to halt indigenous slavery. Islamic slave trading continued into the twentieth century. On this point, the Government and the SUM were in agreement. Thus, the Government turned to the SUM to establish a Freed Slaves' Home. The Home became the Lucy Memorial Freed Slaves' Home, in honor of Lucy Guinness Kumm who had raised money for the Home and worked for its establishment. Lucy Kumm died in 1906; the Home was built in Rumusha in 1909. The government insisted on the presence of women missionaries before allowing the Home to open. Thus, Mary McNaught and Clara Haigh from Britain and the Stewart sisters from South Africa came to Rumasha to run the Home while David Forbes headed an effort to educate blind children.

The Lucy Memorial Freed Slaves' Home became a means through which the SUM entered the educational system of Nigeria. Hans Vischer set up the system in 1909 and as an ex-CMS missionary had no problem in including missionary establishments within the system. A position in the educational system aided the SUM's goal of creating an indigenous African Church. Education was a key to an educated indigenous clergy and laity, which would be able to rule itself and recruit its own members. In time there were thirteen denomination in the middle belt of Nigeria. Some of them are the Church of Christ in the Sudan among the Tiv, The Christian Reformed Church in Nigeria, the Reformed Church of Christ in Nigeria, and the Evangelical Reformed Church of Christ in Nigeria.

The SUM had to take into account the still influential Hausa people. The term Hausa can refer to either the language or a people who identify themselves as Hausa. The language is spoken indigenously by a number of people, Hausa and otherwise, spread across the savanna along the far north of Nigeria from its western boundary eastward to Borno and even into much of southern Niger. The Hausa people comprise those who share cultural practices and who were and in some cases still are ruled through Islamic emirates. These emirates are still significant in the Twenty-First Century. Typically each emirate had a major town, housing the ruling nobles. This royal group controlled the administrative, judicial, religious, and military organization of the state. Trade served as a reason for the state. At the time of British control in the early Twentieth Century, some of these emirates were major urban centers: Kano, Zaria, Sokoto, and Katsina for example. These emirates not only had central markets but a complex system of government and trade as well as craft specialists and various organization. Indigenous Hausa peoples had intermarried with conquering Fulani. These Fulani had used Islam as an organizing force, revitalizing an older Islamic base, largely limited to the rulers.

In addition to mastering the culture, language, and history of the Hausa, missionaries had to become familiar with the Kanuri of Bornu. These people also had a long history in Nigeria, going back to the Fifteenth Century. The conquered local people set up a capital in the area, and then warred with the Fulani. They held off the Fulani, who were on a jihad to conquer them. Like the Hausa-Fulani, the Kanuri are Muslims and share much in common with their neighbors. Missionaries had to note the similarities and distinctions between these peoples and work with them.

Additionally, the SUM had to deal with the multi-ethnic nature of the Middle Belt. There are many religions in the area, in addition to Islam and Christianity. Traditional religions present a bewildering array of customs and traditions. The area runs from the Cameroon Highlands to the Niger River Valley. The groups include people not only of different languages but even language groups from Afro-Asiatic through Chadic. In all there may be 100 separate linguistic and ethnic groups in the region. Since Colonial Law prohibited missionaries from working in Muslim areas and with Muslims, these were the people among whom the missionaries worked directly. The Lucy Memorial Feed Slaves' Home provided them with experience useful in working with these groups. They learned how to establish schools, medical units, and churches, thus helping to separate Muslims and other peoples from each other.

The Freed Slaves' Home also enabled the SUM to help pioneer special education in Nigeria. The Reverend David Forbes and his wife began educating a few blind girls at the Home in Rumasha in 1916 (Forbes 1917, Olusanya 1966). One of the students, a Miss Milkatu, became proficient in Braille and began transcribing material into Hausa Braille. She also became an assistant teacher. Thus, the Home enabled the SUM to reach the many disabled people in Nigeria and aid them in living useful lives. Additionally the Home began teaching deaf children about the same time.

Not surprisingly visitors began to come to the Home, adding it to things to see in Northern Nigeria. The following quotation gives some of the flavor of the Home. It accompanies a photograph of Children in the Freed Slaves' Home in Rumasha. The photo is 100 x 76 mm.

> Next day we stopped at a place called Rumasha, where the Sudan United Mission have a station. Last year the Government handed over to them all the little slave-children who had, from time to time, been rescued. Although we do everything possible to stamp out the slave trade, there is still a good deal of it going on in a small way. . . . The kids seem to be wonderfully well cared for, and are as fat as butter. They are of all ages up to 16, and the bigger ones are made to work, either in the fields, or at various trades. There is an extraordinary mixture of them, and many come from the wildest and most remote parts of the country. (Bell 1910, October 3)

The Freed Slaves' Home enabled the SUM to distinguish itself from other Protestant missions, while building an ecumenical union of evangelicals. It also provided them with a variation on an older pattern, one which enabled missionaries to achieve success in the midst of hostility.

> It was the introduction of the school and the "white man's medicine" that began to attract Africans to the church. The original response to the school was to reject it since it too was associated with other aspects of European culture, most notably Christianity which had come to be viewed with suspicion. Initially people left it to the abandoned slaves and social outcasts to test the new institutions before sending their own children. Even then only the weak, the lazy, or the naughty ones were sent to school. The presence of social outcasts, in particular in the school, and therefore also in the church since one could not go to the school without being a church-goer, made both institutions very unpopular with the rest of the society. To ensure constant attendance the

children were bribed with sweets for themselves and salt to take back home. Through school it was possible to shape the faith and world-view of the young people who were not yet old enough to have accepted the traditional norms of society. (Sam Kobia, "Denominations in Africa," *The Ecumenical Review* 53 (3) 2001, p. 295)

If it true that, as Kobia noted, "The school and the mission station came to provide a 'safe space' for those who were otherwise considered worthless in the society," then these institutions appealed to those who were on the lower rungs of society and were generally enemies of their Muslim rulers. The social outcasts in particular could not help but embrace an institution which recognized them as people worthy of respect. Thus, they made very good 'Christians'. It was even truer that those in the Freed Slaves' Home were even more loyal than most Christians. They were loyal evangelicals, whatever specific denomination they would eventually become. Kobia also notes that the missionaries became part of the colonial establishment, an issue we pursue further in the next chapter. The SUM carefully pursued Lugard's policy in educating the people at the Lucy Memorial Freed Slaves' Home. Indeed the Home was a feature of Lugard's policy before he came to Nigeria. It was a component of British policy at least as early as the late Eighteenth and early Nineteenth Centuries.

Patrick Webb provides an interesting glimpse into the situation in Gambia in *Guests of the Crown: Convicts and Liberated Slaves in McCarthy Island, The Gambia*. The British abolished slavery in 1808. They then began what became a century long battle to end the international slave trade and local trade in slaves in Africa. Part of that battle was to find a refuge area, a home, for the freed slaves within the African area. The founding of Sierra Leone was not a complete solution. Thus, the British attempted to set up a sort of home on McCarthy Island in the Gambia.

Lord Lugard had ideas for a Freed Slaves' Home in Uganda, before coming to Nigeria. He wrote in his Diary:

I wrote today to the C.M.S. proposing that they should take spiritual charge of freed slaves whom I intended to locate on Company's shambas in various districts. I suggested they should form new Mission Stations in Uganda, and that these should be near to my free-slave shambas. I asked *where* they would like to build that I might get my shambas close by. *Vide* the letter (in book) which is an important one. It is ridiculous all these missionaries being huddled up here, and then talking of putting a question in the House because I would not let them go to Busoga at the moment they wished to do so. And yet in spite of repeated verbal hints and queries and suggestions, they will not even form Mission Stations in Uganda itself. Ashe congratulated me strongly on my success with the Islam. (Margery Perham, ed., *The Diaries of Lord Lugard*. Volume 3: Northwestern University Press. Evanston, IL. 1959, p. 276.)

This was an idea Lugard mentioned a number of times. He was finally able to find a mission organization he could trust in Nigeria—the SUM—and one which, in turn, would see the opportunity cooperation with Lugard would give them for mission expansion.

There was also the example of the Freed Slaves' Home at Kumasi in the Gold Coast, established in 1896. It must be remembered that in cooperating with Lugard, the SUM was carrying on an old alliance to abolish slavery. Mission groups had been deeply involved in the British abolition movement. Sierra Leone itself was a missionary settlement to bring about an African society free of slavery and for freed slaves. Missionaries saw the end of slavery, including local slavery in Africa, as part of repairing the harm brought about by the European slave trade. In addition to providing compensation to slave owners for freeing slaves, missionaries provided homes for slaves.

The role of the Basel Mission Society in the Gold Coast (Ghana) is especially important in this respect, and Peter Haenger has provided an insightful study into the social dynamics of dependency in the Gold Coast and the role of the Basel Mission in ending slavery and debt bondage well before the formal onset of British colonialism in 1874 [Peter Haenger, *Slave and Slave Holders on the Gold Coast* (2000)]. Asante resisted the abolition of slavery until colonial annexation in 1896. Basel missionary, F. A. Ramseyer, followed the invading British force to Asante and set up the beginnings of the Basel mission church in Kumase. Mr. and Mrs. Ramseyer took in freed slaves and provided a home for them, clothed them, and guided them on the road to conversion. Today the major Presbyterian Church in Adum, Kumase, is popularly referred to as "Ramseyer." (http://www.bmpix.org/visip_emmanuel/chapter_10.htm)

The SUM, then, was carrying on a tradition in mission work and in mission-government cooperation. Along the way it was fulfilling its own goal of seeking to find ways to halt the spread of Islam. It was caring for those who had been enslaved by Muslims and providing opportunities for better lives separate from Muslims. As part of the establishment it had the power of the British raj behind its actions. So long as it provided the kind of education the British Colonial Government approved, there would be little trouble.

In a pamphlet entitled *The Lucy Memorial Freed Slaves' Home* the central role of the Home is made clear. First the SUM states its clear objective: "To win for Christ the heathen nations of the Sudan, numbering many millions, who are rapidly going over to Mohammedanism for the lack of Christian workers." Then it states under the heading "The Lucy Memorial Freed Slaves' Home"—

> The formation of the Sudan United Mission will ever be associated with the burning missionary zeal and consecrated life of the late Mrs. Karl Kumm, the last years of whose life were devoted to the organization of an effort to carry the Gospel to the Sudan, the last great neglected country in the world. By voice and pen, both gifted in a marvelous degree, she endeavored to make known the claims of this dark land. It was in her last effort that the Master she so lovingly served called her to higher service in His presence. (n.d., p. 3)

The SUM decided to found the Freed Slaves' Home as a "lasting memorial of her life and work." It is clear that the Home was indeed to be a wedge for the SUM into the Nigerian missions. Karl Kumm suggested that the SUM amend its statement of the Freed Slaves' Home in the following manner.

> Although the Mission has been encouraged in the highest quarters to establish a Freed Slaves' Home in Northern Nigeria, conflicting reports as to the number of slaves being freed now in Northern Nigeria make it appear advisable that other branches of usefulness should be added to this Memorial Home, in the shape of an educational institution and an industrial home. These latter branches are to take the place of the Freed Slaves' Home, should the supply of Freed Slaves fail. (n.d., p. 5)

The pamphlet goes on to quote extracts from Lugard's 1905-1906 Report (Par. 50, January 1907). Lugard notes the very active slave trade taking place throughout Bornu. The British were taking serious measures to halt the trade and freed 174 slaves in the first quarter of 1906.

Consequently, "The Freed Slaves' Home in Bornu is overcrowded with liberated children, and has been enlarged; and it has now been found necessary to start a Freed Slaves' Village for adults as well." Lugard fears the continuation of the trade unless the Germans and French close the markets. He also notes that those enslaved are "chiefly the very lowest type of cannibals."

Lugard goes on to discuss slave trading in Muri Province (Par. 80). He mentions that the famine contributed to the slave trade. People sold children to obtain food. In passing, he mentions an incident in which slave traders appear to capsize their canoe intentionally, killing twelve of the twenty-two children on board. One slave trader was captured by a crocodile. This latter story of young children loaded into canoes and in danger of or actually drowning captured the missionary imagination. Variations appear in their writings over the years.

The next section of the Lucy pamphlet is entitled "The Open Sore of Africa—Slave Raiding." Karl Kumm is the author, and he makes clear that the SUM views its mission as a Crusade to stop the flow of Islam. He opens his contribution with a quotation from the Qu'ran, "If they neighbour will not be converted, enslave him." He then briefly recounts the story of the fall of Kuka, then capital of the Bornu Empire. Rabbah stormed the city, burned it, and captured its people and enslaved them. He sums up the cruel inhumanity of the "Arab Muslims" in this passage,

> There was a little boy amongst their number, who had known a happy home life in Kuka. Now all those he loved had been killed, and he was tied with some other boys and began the long trying march. No kind word, little food, and much beating, mile after mile they struggled along. In the evening some village was reached, and tired out they lay down to sleep. Next morning the journey was continued, and thus, day after day, until Dikoa was reached. (Kumm n.d., pp. 8-9)

The story continues with the boy being sold to a rich Arab. This Arab put him to work in the fields. When this small boy could not keep up with the work, he was whipped. When his health gave way, the owner sold him to Hausa merchant. This man took him to Lokoja. He worked with the trader, who did not treat him well. Finally, the young boy escaped and found himself at the home of a white man. That young boy stayed with the SUM and the missionaries named him Tom. Tom appears frequently in SUM writings and was their first convert.

Kumm provides other stories. He mentions young girls taken in slavery and sent to harems in Turkey and other areas of the Muslim world. Finally, he brings it all back to the role of the Home in the overall crusade against Islam.

> What more fitting memorial to the life work of the late Mrs. Kumm could be devised than a home for those rescued from the awful fate of slavery—a home where Christian love would reign, and the gospel of redeeming grace be taught. (Kumm, n.d., pp. 15-16)

Chapter Three

Expatriate Society, Lugard, Indirect Rule, and Ending Slavery

Primary among the criticisms that third-world scholars and "radical" social scientists have directed against applied social sciences in general and social anthropology in particular has been their alleged failures to study the colonial context in which much of its field work has been carried out (Cf. Asad, 1975; Lewis, 1973, for examples.) Although these critics usually exaggerate their arguments and typically do not prove that early scholars were either overt or covert racists, it is true, nonetheless, that social scientists have paid relatively little attention to the colonial milieu, Condominas's (1973) *preterrain.*

A number of scholars, including Pitt (1976) and Stavenhagen (1971), have urged that social scientists "study upwards" in order to discover the social and cultural foundations of the colonizing agency in the contact situation, which determine its motivations and constrain its actions. Failure to do so entails serious theoretical and methodological consequences because it both narrows the range of societies among which we are able to make comparisons and masks systematic bias. Although I have been deeply concerned with the problem of systematic bias (Salamone, 1976a, b), I address the issue of describing and analyzing a colonial society, of "studying up." The reason is quite simple. It is necessary *to* know the nature of a systematic source of bias before deciding on whether and how to control it.

Furthermore, the value of studying expatriate societies transcends its significant relationship to problems of the validity and reliability of social science research because expatriate societies are only one transform of plural societies, one of many possible concrete manifestations of deeper underlying structural principles. Before social science can succeed in uncovering these structural principles, further empirical research and clearer conceptualization of the problem are needed. Beidelman (1974: 235-36) states the situation succinctly:

> Anthropologists tend to neglect those groups nearest themselves, and in the scurry to conduct relevant research, a broad area of great theoretical interest has been passed by. Almost no attention was ever paid by anthropologists to the study of colonial groups such as administration, missionaries, or traders. . . . Anthropologists may have spoken about studying total societies, but they did not seem to consider their compatriots as subjects for wonder and analysis. . . . Colonial structures may be viewed as variants of a tar broader type, that of the complex bureaucratic organization.

Beidelman's perceptive categorization of expatriate colonial society as a subtype or variant of Weber's "complex bureaucratic organization" parallels M. G. Smith's (1969: 434) contention that colonial society is but one important variant of the plural society. Smith's (ibid.: 444-45) further discussion regarding the types of pluralism suggests a useful research approach: Structural pluralism consists in the differential incorporation of connectivities segregated as social sections and characterized by institutional divergences. Cultural pluralism consists in variable institutional diversity without corresponding collective segregation. Social pluralisms involves the organization of institutionally dissimilar collectivities in corporate sections or segments whose boundaries demarcate distinct communities and systems of social action. The differential incorporation that institutes structural pluralism is found only in societies where institutionally diverse collectivities are set apart as corporate social sections of unequal status and resources. In these conditions, if the ruling sections form a numerical minority of the aggregate, we find the plural society in the classic form described by Furnival.

Social scientists have described Furnival's classic plural society, colonial society, in works of greater or lesser detail. They have failed to provide adequate descriptions, however, of the workings of colonial society in non-settler communities. Furthermore, these descriptions, with rare exceptions, tend to be outsiders' views which typically describe either the subordinate sections of the plural society or contact areas. Rarely does any social scientist analyze the dominant stratum. Indeed, it is rather suggestive that, on the whole, novelists such as Paul Theroux, Joyce Carey, and George Orwell have offered the best descriptions of expatriate societies, ones that compel emotional assent.

Beidelman's (1974: 235-36) recommendation that scholars focus attention on dominant segments of colonial society, using a Weberian analytic framework, can be profitably combined with a judicious use of Smith's model of structural pluralism. Significantly, these Weberian approaches not *only* do not logically exclude the notion of process, they profit by it. They do so because the corporate segments of the plural society are always in real or potential conflict, and, at best, any equilibrium is tenuous (Kuper, 1969: 462, 465, especially 470,475). In addition, there is a dynamic conflict within each section, one that has been, unfortunately, virtually ignored within the literature.

There is need, then, to focus on one transform of the plural society, the non-settler colonial society. There is even greater need to focus on the dominant segment of the society, the expatriate component. That segment is itself one variety of Weber's bureaucratic type. Any solution to the problem of kinds of plural societies and their underlying processes can only result from the application of theoretically derived concepts to empirical situations carefully chosen to permit the observation of the interaction of relevant variables.

By definition, colonial society is composed of an expatriate ruling class and a subordinated indigenous class. Of course each of these classes is comprised of a number of layers. Expatriates, for example, were made of rulers, civil servants, missionaries, temporary workers, merchants, assorted businessmen, wives, and even visiting academics. Settler colonies had further distinctions. These expatriates formed a dissimilar group who often disagreed, coming from different social classes in Europe.

It is clear that colonialism had profound effects on world history, including the creation of numerous ethnic identities in the colonized world. Therefore, simply lumping together subjected colonial peoples confuses attempts to understand the colonial scene. There were differences in ranking among favored and less favored people in the colonial system. Colonial reality virtually demanded that those in power, the expatriate ruling class, work with favored indigenous people over less favored ones. In the British system that was the underlying meaning of Indirect Rule.

In Nigeria, Ghana, and other British colonies under Indirect Rule expatriates over represented the upper middle class in Britain. In social class origins and value, they presented a false and outdated side of British culture. Unsurprisingly, they structured their contacts with indigenous peoples along carefully pre-selected routes. They valued, for example, proper aristocratic behavior, favoring those groups, such as the Fulani, whom they considered more refined in demeanor and nobler in tradition.

It is significant here to be aware that the sacred tenets of indirect rule required local financial support for all local governmental functions, including education. Additionally, in Nigeria at least, the British found it useful to posit an innate hostility between Islam and Christianity, between Western and Islamic education and practices and significantly between democracy and adherence to tradition. However, among those who were clearly not Muslims and who were freed slaves, the British encouraged missionaries to evangelization, including founding hospitals and schools. Heussler's (1968) *The British in Northern Nigeria* is, perhaps, the best single source dealing with the establishment and evolution of British rule in Northern Nigeria. It has the added virtue of dealing with the expatriate section of colonial society in a manner that sheds light on its members' motivations and actions. Heussler manages to recreate the colonial milieu in his work, enabling the reader to empathize with the historical characters and situations depicted. Of the takeover, he (1968: 13) says:

> In 1900, when she assumed formal responsibility for Northern Nigeria, Britain's knowledge and experience of the area were remarkably slight. A handful of British nationals had had extensive trading experience in the new Protectorate's southerly regions along the Niger and Benue and a few had made brief excursions into the northern parts on various missions, commercial, religious, scholarly, and political.

There were, therefore, three major categories of people with knowledge and interests in the north—politicians, missionaries, and merchants. Politicians wished to keep rivals out of Nigeria. In the northern regions that essentially meant the French. Missionaries desired to convert "pagans" and Muslims to Christianity. In addition, they were filled with less clearly defined goals. Their desire, however, to keep the French out of the north was very clear. Similarly, merchants were interested in carrying on trade in a congenial atmosphere. Consequently, they feared and opposed French expansion into the northern areas of Nigeria. Whatever differences existed among members of these groups, they were united in their resolve to keep the French out of the north. Therefore, however reluctantly, the British assumed administrative responsibility for Northern Nigeria in 1900. They were determined to rule with a minimum number of Europeans and cost. That goal led to the promulgation of policies which often conflicted with the desires of missionaries and merchants, whose members had preceded British administrators to the north and, to a great extent, created the circumstances which required their presence there.

The role of Sir George Goldie (1846-1925) in the annexation process has been well-documented (Flint, 1960) and it is with some justice that he is termed "the founder of Nigeria." Certainly few people originally shared his perception that British annexation of land along the Niger River was indispensable to commerce's security. He came to that conclusion in 1877, a time when imperialism was unpopular in the United Kingdom. Shortly before, in 1868 the British had removed their consular official from the Niger in response to a June 1865 resolution of the House of Commons calling for an end to British involvement in West Africa.

Lack of governmental and popular support for his opinions did not prevent Goldie from capitalizing on his organizational abilities nor from creating circumstances, which forced the government's hand. Goldie's first steps were to eliminate the cutthroat competition among trading companies that had led to the stagnation of trade. In Goldie's eyes competition had forestalled the advance of trade to the upper Niger regions where the Muslim empires were. It was Goldie's ultimate aim to secure control of the entire Niger Valley for Great Britain. At the time, there were foreign powers from Senegal to the Nile Valley.

He understood that such a situation could not long exist. Therefore, he moved rapidly and by 1879 had formed the United African Company, the first of a series of amalgamations for trading companies Goldie organized, which he hoped to use for imperialistic purposes. His attempts to receive a charter, however, were failures for either economic or political reasons. Germany's entry into the colonial sweep-stakes in 1884, however, altered the situation.

Goldie's timely purchase of two French Niger trading companies enabled Great Britain to state at the West African Conference in Berlin (1884-1885) that she controlled the trade of the Niger Basin. By 1886, it had become obvious to Great Britain that Goldie's trading company could not equally compete with France and Germany. On behalf of a private company Goldie had been concluding treaties with local rulers while French and German agents were acting on behalf of their respective governments. Therefore, in July 1886 the British government chartered the Royal Niger Company.

Surprisingly, the company was given political powers without losing its economic privileges. It was nominally under the control of the office of the Secretary of State for the Colonies. In actual practice it carried out its directive to govern, preserve social order, and to protect the territory of treaty chiefs in relative autonomy. Its mandate gave the right to exercise authority over British subjects and foreigners in its territory. In effect, Goldie became the first British administrator of what was to become Northern Nigeria. Although he did not become the actual governor of the Royal Niger Company until 1895, he was its de facto ruler from its beginning. As such, he set the pattern for policies later followed by Lord Lugard, the first High Commissioner of Northern Nigeria. These policies included the elimination of slave raiding; religious tolerance, including the discouragement of missionary activity; and ruling through local rulers in conformity with "native laws and customs." In all but name, Goldie developed what Lugard later named "indirect rule" or the "dual mandate."

That he and Lugard governed in a similar manner is not surprising. After all, Lugard served under Goldie in Nigeria in 1894. His race to Nikki in Borgu and the subsequent treaty he negotiated enabled the British to beat the French to the area. Furthermore, his role in forming the West African Frontier Force was instrumental in keeping peace with France and bringing about the 1898 convention that together with that of 1893 with Germany ended the struggle for control of the Niger. Goldie had negotiated these treaties and Lugard was a trusted lieutenant. Additionally, however, the structural conditions under which these two men governed were virtually identical. They had to administer a vast area of about one-half million square miles with few trained personnel and little money. The area itself was composed of a large number of ethnic groups organized in a wide variety of political structures, ranging from large empires to households. Furthermore, slave raiding by the Fulani kingdoms on the southern "pagans" posed a major problem to the preservation of law and order and the peaceful propagation of trade.

When the British Government assumed formal control of Northern Nigeria on 1 January 1900, at Lokoja, it gave to Lugard all the problems that Goldie had attempted to overcome. In fact, it was primarily the result of Goldie's efforts that the British Government even recognized that problems existed. A major cause for that recognition was Goldie's defeat of the emirs of Nupe and Ilorin in 1897, a result of their persistent slave raiding. Fuller realization of the significance of the circumstances in Northern Nigeria led to British assumption of the political and territorial powers of the Royal Niger Company.

Goldie's policies resulted in an alliance between merchants and politicians. Although their interests were not identical, they coincided sufficiently enough to promote cooperation. Similarly, European missionaries had advocated a direct governmental role in protecting their interests. They had been upset with Goldie's separation of religion from politics and trade. There was little patience in the missionary community for his conciliatory gestures toward Muslim rulers. In fact, European missionaries attributed much of his anti-missionary attitude to his being a Jew.

Bishop Samuel Crowther, however, was not so impatient. Crowther was a Yoruba Missionary who, unfortunately, became the focal point of an attack on African agents for the Church Mission Society (CMS) by European missionaries. These attacks were led by a group of missionaries who became known as the Sudan Party.

Members of the party were in favor of "pure, simple, primitive Christianity" presented through indigenous symbols (Owoh, 1971: 279). They believed in going directly to the people over the heads of their "despotic" Fulani rulers. To do so, they adopted the *tobe,* the traditional dress of the people, and spoke fluent Hausa. In that language they were eloquently outspoken on matters of religion, morals, and politics. Their presuppositions regarding the peaceful nature of non-Fulani and their readiness to accept Christianity added to their fervor. In fact, they believed that only the bigotry of their Fulani rulers prevented the Hausa from immediate conversion to Christianity.

They never understood that their adoption of the *tobe* caused excitement among the populace because they thought the missionaries were converting to Islam. Owoh (ibid.: 298) states, "The adoption of the *tobe* by European missionaries, then, was greeted with excitement by the local people because it brought the rich white missionaries within approachable distance." The failure of the members of the Sudan Party to live like Muslims, however, and the threat they posed to traditional Islamic teachers and the emirs created great political problems. Furthermore, the Sudan Party's opposition to African clergy had serious repercussions, with many Sierra Leonians turning on the C.M.S. and condemning it to Hausa authorities. In addition, that policy split the northern and southern Nigerian churches for years.

Given both the manner in which the Sudan Party had conducted itself and its anti-Fulani stance, it is not surprising that Lugard and his successors were cautious in their relationships with missionaries. Circumstances forced them to rule through those very Islamic rulers whom the missionaries were condemning. Lugard desired to use as little force as possible in establishing British control. Missionaries posed a serious threat to his plans. He, however, was the son of missionaries and far from anti-missionary in his sentiments. Furthermore, he was quite aware of the contributions that voluntary agencies could make to the development of Northern Nigeria, and at a very small cost to the government.

Such was the situation in 1903, the third year of Lugard's period of rule in Northern Nigeria, the year in which he defeated both Kano and Sokoto.

Early Expatriate Society in Northern Nigeria

There are a number of characteristics that distinguish expatriate societies from similar groups. Most obvious is the fact that expatriates come from another area, one that provides support, and one to which they ostensibly can return, sooner or later, when they finish their tour of duty. Indeed, "tour of duty" is quite an accurate description of expatriate perception of the definition of the situation—as Van Baal (1972: 87) makes clear in his own case. He went to the Netherlands East Indies because it was his moral duty to do so in order to serve mankind. Although further empirical work is necessary, it is probable that expatriates are not demographically or in value-orientation representative of their home areas. Thus, they tend to present a false and outdated version of their home societies to indigenous people. Furthermore, their contacts with those people are along pre-selected routes, congruent with their occupation of dominant power positions. Finally, although colonial officials, missionaries, indigenous staff, recognized representative of local people, servants, and the occasional anthropologist frequently differed bitterly, there were a number of instances in which overt disagreements were not tolerated, for each segment within the expatriate stratum had too much at stake in the preservation of the structure to endanger its maintenance.

The actual religious, demographic, and political situations into which the British came are important to an understanding of the patterns that they established. To put it concretely: without an understanding of the situation in which the British consolidated their rule it is impossible to understand the structure and functioning of the non-settler colonial society that Nigeria became.

In 1910 there were 338 Europeans in Northern Nigeria, 120 of whom were merchants (Ajayi, Ab/p. *12/2:14)*. In 1911 there were 678 Europeans in a population of 8,115,981. They constituted .00835 percent of the population, a figure that increased slightly in the census of 1921 to .01138 percent and to .01595 percent in 1931. The actual proportion of Europeans in the population in 1921 and 1931 was 1,168 of 10,259,993 and 1,825 of 11,434,924. Perhaps a more graphic illustration of the relative size of the two communities is given by a comparison of the number of Europeans and Nigerians per square mile. In 1911, there were .00265 Europeans per square mile compared with 31.74 Nigerians. In 1921 the figures were .00447 compared with 39.33. 1931's figures showed .0069958 to 40.58 (Brooke, 1933: 1). In short, the expatriate community was a face to face one, one that was both absolutely and relatively small.

Although Brooke (1933: 66) listed the north as essentially Islamic, the figures he gave for Sokoto cast doubt on his reliability in this matter. He reports, for example, only 126,505 "animists" among indigenous non-Hausa people in a population of 254,324 and 15,312 among a population of 1,106,649 Hausa. My own research (Salamone, 1974), centered on the Yauri region of Sokoto, and that of Barkow (1970), however, casts serious doubt on the accuracy of these figures. Much more probable is the analysis found in Trimingham's (Ab: P12/1:8:18-19) report to the CMS and MMS.

In it he stresses the rapidity of Islam's twentieth century expansion and the difference between Islam among the Kanuri, Yoruba, and Hausa. Among the Kaouri, Islam is deep and of long duration. Whereas it is a religion among the Yoruba, it is a civilization among the Hausa. The rapid spread of Islam in Hausaland, from 5 percent of the population in 1900 to 80 percent in 1950, resulted from British policy favoring Islam. After the British conquest, Islam was no longer viewed by the Hausa as the religion of the Fulani. Rather they viewed it as an alternate civilization, useful in opposition to western influence, and one honored by British policy.

One of the things to make clear is that until the British occupation Islam in West Africa was largely an aristocratic religion, professed by the ruling class who only attempted to impose it on their subjects in the early stages of the end of the 18th and beginning of the 19th centuries (Trimingham, Ab:P12/1:8:19).

The distinction between sacred and secular, deeply imbedded in western culture, is antithetical to the Islamic state structure. Ironically, the Christian missionary has been one of the prime factors working toward distinguishing the two. That separation, which Trimingham (Ab:PI2/ 1:8:31) sums up as the "individual morality" of the missionary, is viewed by Muslims and non-Muslims in Northern Nigeria as a menace to societal stability.

The early situation, then was one in which there were very few expatriates. Originally, almost half of these were traders, who had exercised quasi-political functions before the establishment of the protectorate. The minuscule force of government officials was dependent on securing local cooperation for their efforts. Although missionaries could not cavalierly be excluded from the north, their work could be hindered, for they clearly presented a hindrance to the effective and smooth cooperation of Islamic officials. Given the face-to-face nature of the British community, much of the interaction takes on clear cut characteristics, typical of many of the societies which anthropologists are more accustomed to studying. In brief, conflicts clearly reveal underlying structural characteristics. Thus, Rattray's (1934) hypothesis regarding indirect rule assumes added dimension when judged against Dr. Walter Miller's case history presented in the following section. Basically, Rattray (1934: 26.27) suggested

> . . . that, thirty or forty years ago, when the science of anthropology was still in its infancy, had the European conquerors of Northern Nigeria encountered such a state of society [that of West Africans] . . . they would have had neither the knowledge, nor the means, nor the time to have comprehended it, and, in consequence, Indirect Rule, as we understand it would have been almost impossible of introduction. The complexity of a so-called "primitive" tribal society would have been unintelligible to them, the intimately related social units would have seemed lacking in cohesion, nothing worthy of the name constitution or state would have been apparent. . . . It was inevitable . . . that the point of view, the only point of view, ever put forward to the British Government in those early days must have been that of this upper-ruling class—this alien aristocracy, the Fulani, this foreign minority among the millions of inarticulate subjects over whom for a hundred years these invaders had wielded what was probably only a very nominal suzerainty.

In short, the end result of Indirect Rule was the strengthening of Fulani rule in a way predictable through the application of Smith's theory of the plural society.

Indeed, Palmer's (1934: 37-48) response to Rattray is revealingly instructive. He accused Rattray of being pro-Hausa and anti-Fulani, concluding his attack by citing an un-named "learned member of the Nigerian Legislature" who complained "that he could never find out the difference between an Anthropologist and a Secretary for Native Affairs." Both, according to Palmer, were troublesome creatures who threaten a carefully balanced governing arrangement.

The point is that colonial society in Nigeria was quite complex. It was not a case of "the British" vs. "the Africans." Quite clearly neither "the British" nor "the Africans" formed a monolithic group. Rattray made explicit the alliance between colonial officials and Fulani elite. In addition, he demonstrated the simplified selective perception which enable the British to rule an area notable for its ethnographic complexity. Quite simply, British political officers accepted the Fulani's idealized version of political reality, one that those whom the Fulani conquered never accepted. Furthermore, because of its advantage in easing their rule, the British political corps solidified Fulani rule at the very time it was most in danger of collapsing.

Because of their personal contacts with indigenous peoples, missionaries, anthropologists, and secretaries for native affairs were in excellent positions to challenge this mutually convenient arrangement between Fulani and British colonial officers and its consequent distortion of reality. In turn, of course, missionaries, anthropologists, and secretaries for native affairs had perceptual biases of their own related to the interests and allegiances of their positions. As a consequence, competing versions of reality entered the colonial arena. Furthermore, although colonial officials had power to limit internal opposition, those whom they opposed frequently brought countervailing power to bear in Great Britain. It is, in fact, this extension of disputes and the resulting appeal to power ultimately residing in the metropolitan center that makes the concept of the "expatriate society" a useful tool.

The Hausaland Mission

It is simple to comprehend colonial policy regarding missionaries. The general picture has been presented in a number of places (Cf. Owoh,

1971: Crampton, 1967; Ayandele, 1966; and Galloway, 1960). The general pattern was composed of the following. First, there was the separation of politics from religion, a policy stemming from Goldie's days. Equally important, on the missionary side, was the "Sudan Party's" break with earlier missionary policy and its consequent downgrading of African missionaries. As a result of ignoring Crowther's policy, British missionaries began to emphasize individual conversions, rather than focusing on the community. This emphasis on the individual versus his community was one of the features of missionary activity that caused friction between missionary and administrator. Another characteristic was mission belief in the easy conversion of Hausa, leading to fierce mission/Fulani hostility.

Quite predictably, each phase of mission/government interaction was one of disagreement and conflicting perceptions of their proper respective roles. Simply, missionaries believed that the government should help them to convert Muslims; the spread of British military power entailed the expansion of Christianity (Cf. Letter of Tugwell, Miller and Burgin *to* Lugard, 14 February 1901: CMS G3/A9/01). It was just that feeling, natural to the Fulani who had reached power via the *jihad,* that the British wished to combat, for it threatened to attack the core of the British-Fulani clientage relationship. At the same time, however, the British were honor bound to protect the missionaries, for, as Crampton (1967: 45) pointed out, an insult to one European was interpreted as an insult to all. Furthermore, although many officers were not themselves favorably disposed toward Christianity, and many members of the colonial secretariat were even anti-missionary Unitarians (Crampton, 1967: 55), Christianity was a symbol of the British Empire and many missionaries had powerful interests at home.

The correspondence of the Hausaland Mission from the year 1903 illustrates these generalizations in a specific case. In order to appreciate the importance of the Hausaland Mission to Northern Nigeria's social history it is necessary to provide a brief historical sketch of previous missionary work. More complete accounts are available in Ayandele (1966: 116.52) and Ajayi (1965), among others. In 1855, T. J. Bowen, an American Southern Baptist, made the first serious missionary attempt to found a northern station at Ilorin. More promising, however, was the work of the Yoruba missionary, S. A. Crowther. Crowther's emphasis on community, rather than individual, conversion was less threatening to the emirs than efforts at individual conversion European missionaries favored so highly, an approach that ripped the convert from his or her traditional community. Proof of the efficacy of his method was the ease with which he obtained permission to open mission stations from allegedly anti-Christian Fulani emirs. In 1857 he opened stations at Lokoja, Egga, and Kipo Hill, all with the permission of Nupe emirs. Shortly thereafter Bida, Ilorin and Gwandu granted permission for stations to be opened in their territories. The Fulani rulers did not merely tolerate these stations; they welcomed them.

Unfortunately, European missionaries undermined these promising early African efforts to convert the north. It was unfortunate because European efforts were predicated on an interpretation of reality that was as simplistic as that of most colonial officers. It erred, however, on the opposite side. European missionaries were strongly anti-Fulani and believed that the Hausa as distinct from their Fulani rulers, were eager to embrace Christianity. They opposed Crowther's conciliatory policy and processed for the immediate conversion of northerners, in the process ignoring the Muslim emirs.

It is essential to note that those European missionaries were strongly imperialistic. Not *only* did they believe that the CMS should dispense with African agents, such as Crowther, but that it was the duty of Great Britain to protect missionaries and ease their conversion of Muslims and "pagans." At every opportunity, they attempted to force the government's hand on the issue.

G. W. Brooke's Sudan Party (1890-1892) set the pattern for colonial/missionary relations. That party was inspired by Gordon's anti-Mahdist campaign in the Sudan, and the fear that the Mahdi would rise in Nigeria. The CMS sent 11 Cambridge and Oxford graduates to Northern Nigeria, the largest single party they had ever sent to one area. The Sudan Party's attempt at cultural conversion failed miserably. Not only were their premises incorrect, but their protection against disease was tragically inadequate. They were intensely anti-Fulani and perpetuated the myth that all Hausa were nominal Muslims eagerly awaiting the liberation of Christianity, a myth that plagued missionary relationships with northern Nigerians for years.

The ultimate failure of the Sudan Party, ravished by illness and death, only spurred other missionary efforts. In 1891 a Hausa Association was formed in memory of J. A. Robinson of the Sudan Party. The real reason for its foundation was the conversion of Hausa. Goldie encouraged its foundation, for he had begun to appreciate that the government could use

missionaries to build hospitals and promote education and other voluntary activities. Thus, Goldie helped establish that very pattern when he
"gave" one hundred freed slaves to the missions for conversion, encouraging missionary belief that the "Sword of Steel" would go before the
"Sword of Faith." The 1896 Bida War, in missionary eyes, became the
precursor of what was to come.

It was the immediate cause for the 1898 expedition of the Hausaland
Mission to Hausa settlements in Tripoli, for added to missionary hatred
of the Fulani and Islam, was their fear and hatred of French Roman
Catholics who were threatening to take over Northern Nigeria. One of
the men in that party was Dr. Walter Miller, whose missionary career is
itself a commentary on the development of British policy in Northern
Nigeria.

Although Miller's endeavors were in many ways atypical of missionary work, and he personally was at least unique, it is for these reasons
that his work is so important in exposing relationships within the expatriate community that otherwise remain implicit. Miller was one of those
people who had a knack for forcing those who possess "potential" power
into converting it to "actual" power, consequently easing its analysis.

Quite early Miner appreciated the importance of attempting to maintain close ties with the administration, ties which he hoped would facilitate his work, or at least allow him relative freedom in ignoring directives. His peculiar relationship with Lugard deserves a complete analysis,
one beyond the scope of this work. As early as 1899, Miller was lavish
in his praise of the new high commissioner, a son of missionaries. In
turn, Lugard was grateful for Miller's role in gaining the allegiance of
Zaria in 1902, just two years after Miller's arrival. That allegiance allowed Lugard's man to defeat Abadie Nagwananchi of Kontagora and to
consolidate British control of the north. In turn, Lugard allowed Miller
to establish a mission within Zaria itself.

1903 has been chosen as a period to describe relationships because it
is the middle of Lugard's first rule, one in which what was to become
fixed dogma was still fluid necessity. The mission community was en-
tirely male, as Bargery's letters to the CMS director, Baylis, make clear.
Bargery was requesting permission to marry and take his wife to the
mission station. He had been in the northern mission two years and four
months, a period equal to that of anyone else. His arguments in favor of
marriage for missionaries and the assignment of women to the field are
valuable in understanding the mission society of the early days. Person-

ally, he argued, there was a danger of not returning to the field, for his future brother-in-law opposed his missionary work; his fiancee might lose her faith if left in that situation. More generally, there was a need for female nurses and doctors. Men could not do a good deal of work in Nigeria's Islamic areas. Unless women were converted, much of the effort will be wasted. Significantly, Bargery suggested that the resident of Zaria's advice be asked.

The issue was the subject of a torrid debate and Miller sent a memo to the CMS, which sheds light on day to day relations in the north. Briefly, arguments in favor of women in the missions were that there was a general peace, and the Mahdi presented no real problem. Furthermore, roads were improved, and whites were seen on every journey. Because of the general peace and improved transportation, housing was more comfortable, for one could furnish the inside in European fashion while keeping the outside in the "native" style. Miller argued that there certainly was work for women to do. The hospital at Zungeru, for example, needed female nurses beyond the single one who worked there. Most importantly, women were needed to set an example for young children.

The fearfully wicked character of all women, even to the little girls— they are ten times more immoral that [sic] the men—makes it impossible if we want the little lads who are about us to grow up healthy and clean to let them have anything to do with these women. The need for a Christian home as an exemplar led Miller to write that he favored mothers first over wives, an obvious slap at Bargery. That there was, however, a need to prove that married men were not homosexuals, Miller admitted. Furthermore, he grudgingly conceded that some good men might refuse to come to the mission field if their wives were left behind, but that might not be a real loss. There were some arguments against allowing any woman to come to the mission area. Mission life had a pioneer nature to it. Roads were bad from July to October. No schools were yet planned for the foreseeable future. Opposition to missionaries was still strong. Finally, the possibility of loneliness was great, for no band of lady workers was yet possible because of the necessity of offering them protection.

Finally, Miller offered the following regulations pending approval by the committee of the use of female missionaries. There should be at least four women, with reinforcements available. Each woman should be free of organic diseases, "Specially those peculiar to women." None should be under the age of 27 or 28, and at least one should be a "strapping old maid", who should be the group leader. No romances should be encouraged, nor should any publicity be given. Work would consist of elementary work, specifically "in the kindergarten style," and nursing and dispensing.

Quite obviously, Miller preferred unmarried clergy, and the parallels between early CMS stations and later Roman Catholic ones are quite suggestive. His authoritarian role is clearly evident in the virtual open rebellion he caused in 1903. The immediate point at issue was the binding nature of his instructions. These essentially would have given Miller absolute control over all missionaries and their households. Bargery led a successful opposition to his absolute rule. In 1903 there was no permanent station. About 50 people attended services. All seven of the missionaries were university people. Preference for public school graduates with varsity training was a common British trait. The normal tour of duty was two and one-half years, followed by home leave. Relations with the government, which in 1903 meant Lugard, were carefully cultivated. In fact, Miller sent Lugard 19 pages of typed instructions in which he advocated changes in medical, moral and economic areas, with the use of force if needed. He complained of the hostility of government officials, and then he flatly stated that he was going to Kano and Katsina.

This missive upset Lugard, who wrote to Baylis on 5 September to comment on Miller's long memo. In the course of that response a number of important issues were addressed. First, he was not opposed to direct rule, but with the staff and money at his disposal, there was no alternative. Although he did not trust the Fulani, necessity dictated that he work through them. To that end officials familiar with Hausa and local customs were needed. Personally, he favored Christian missions, but progress must be made in conjunction with local conditions. This was not the time to anger the Fulani. In short, stay away from Kano and Katsina (Lugard to Baylis, 5 Sept., 1903, from Surrey). On 27 October he sent Baylis another letter warning that he would not support missionaries in Kano or Katsina with force. Missionaries should stick to pagan zones, for he had given his word to keep them out of Muslim territories. In point of fact, neither statement was true. Lugard had earlier rescued Miller's ill-fated expedition to Kano and would have done so again. Furthermore, he had not promised to keep missionaries out of Islamic areas.

Whereas Miller clearly wanted to work among Hausa only, his colleagues were perfectly willing and eager to go in pairs to villages of non-Hausa. Miller himself visited eight to twelve villages of non-Hausa in two tours of seven days each. In this work, their servants aided the missionaries. Unfortunately, no one has yet analyzed the role of the young male servant in missionary work. Certainly, Miller was quite clear in his hopes that these young men, such as his Audu, would be catalysts in the coming Hausa conversion. Despite his close ties with Audu, Miller still believed in the fact of European superiority to the Hausa, a view he modified in his later life. In 1903, however, the highest praise he could give was that someone had acted "Almost like a white man" (Miller to Baylis, 11 June, 1903, CMS: G3 Ag/07/1903; Nos. 1-42, Reel Number 214).

Neither Miller nor Lugard, despite close ties, was lulled by the other's sincere friendship into misjudging his motives. Miller urged Baylis on 11 June to keep the distinction between the mission and the government clear. Any confusion in the peoples' minds between the two was detrimental. It must be stressed, however, that the relationship between missionaries and government was multiplex. Although missionaries might be a nuisance, they did perform valuable work at low cost to the government. For example, medical work figured quite prominently in the mission. Repeatedly, Druitt's medical skill is praised in letters. Lugard's letter to Hans Vischer, head of education for the Northern provinces (MSS British Empire S76: 11 January, 1914) discussed the complexity of missionary contributions in the field of education. At the beginning, Lugard emphasized the lack of resources at the government's disposal. Missionaries were all too eager to fill the gap. The Ugandan experience, however, marred by Christian rivalry was held to be instructive. Therefore, a number of variables must be checked: the form of the missionary, the teacher, and the consent of the parents. Furthermore, spheres of influence should be established. A hint of a *quid pro quo* is found in Lugard's irritation that Islam was allowed into pagan areas where Christianity was excluded. More ironic is the fact that Palmer had invoked Lugard's Indirect Rule to keep missionaries out of areas where Lugard would have welcomed them. In offering a rare glimpse of his inner thoughts, he wrote:

> . . . purely secular Education divorced from Moral Instruction and from Religion, among races who have not the tradition and the ethical standards which centuries of Christian teaching and environment have produced in Europe, infallibly produces a class of young men and women who lack reverence alike for their parents, their social superiors, their employers, or the Government. They lack self restraint and

control, and they lack the foundation on which all the highest and best work in the world is based whether of public and civic usefulness, or of private incentive and effort.

Consequently, Lugard ordered moral education in the secondary schools. He further ordered contact with the Moral Education League in England and the securing of their publications. In addition, he asked that hours for optional religious education be certified, and that the spheres of influence for various religious missions be established (MSS Brit. Em s76).

The impetus given by Lugard's actions is clearly seen. In 1913, there were 38 mission stations in the Northern provinces. In 1917, there were more than 60, including churches in Kaduna, Zaria, and Jos (Secretary, N. P., to Private Secretary to H. E., Governor-General, 17 January 1918, MSS Brit. Em s76). Lugard, however, did not remain in power long and those who replaced him continued the canonization of Indirect Rule. Their motives may well have been mixed, but as Ayandele (1967: 145-52) rightly argues, missionaries presented political problems and were quick to cause difficulties wherever they went. Miller's expedition to Kano in 1901 was a colossal blunder. Merchants were opposed to missionaries, moreover, because they denounced the liquor trade and the general comportment of merchants.

Ayandele (ibid.) makes clear that the policy of men like Girouard and Temple, however, was anti-missionary because, however much they admired Islamic culture, they were afraid of missionary exposure of their shortcomings. Indirect Rulers had much to hide from the gaze of the British public, through probable revelations by the missionaries to the British press. Many of the Residents were overbearing in their attitudes to the natives and condoned many acts of oppression by the chiefs and emirs. The officials were, in a missionary observer's view, "brave English officers, genial, good natured, but utterly ungodly, all living loose lives, all having women brought to them wherever they are." Missionaries also felt that in the pacification of the territory much bloodshed that could have been avoided, the report of which never reached the Colonial Office, occurred. In places where missionaries were allowed to establish themselves many people who could not obtain redress for wrongs from Residents flocked to missionaries for "advice" (ibid.: 151).

The missionary mentioned in the quotation was, of course, Miller and the implacable opposition he had to the slaughter of Nigerians, exemplified in the Hadeja campaign, earned him the hatred of numerous administrators. In short, under Percy Girouard what had been necessity for Lugard became policy. The response that J. F. Matthews (MSS Afr s783, 27 July, 1924) gave to his brother, Basil Matthews's book *The Clash of Colour* (1926: London, Cargate Press) serves as a clear example of the attitude of colonial officers to outside criticism,

> The difficulty with you righteously indignant once is to put yourselves in our place, to visualize the enormous areas and distances involved, the fewness of communication facilities such as railroads, roads and telegraph wires and (most of all) the attitude and mentality of the inhabitants and the consequent difficulty of effect of one's action on the minds of Englishmen..

Matthews went on to bemoan the result of "half-baked education" on the wrong natives who then exploited their illiterate brothers. That hostile attitude toward those who let the side down was applied against missionaries, anthropologists, and others who publicly deviated from the office line. Although the American anthropologist Oberg worked in East Africa, his (Oberg, 1972: 77-78) comments apply to Northern Nigeria.

> Nothing in my past had prepared me to live within barriers as rigid as those which separated Europeans and natives or to come to terms with the harsh punishment sometimes meted out to natives. . . . In retrospect it is easy to see how such conditions enforce conformity and limit the freedom of the anthropologist. . . . It was in Africa that I first encountered culture shock as a personal problem and, I might add, one which also troubled some of the British colonial officials. However, I had the problem of adjusting to two subcultures: that of British colonial officialdom and that of the native people of Ankole. . . . At the time the government station at Mbarara in the district of Ankole consisted of eight British officials. Life in the station was governed by strict routine. Office hours were from eight to one, then lunch and a siesta until four in the afternoon. I was soon informed that house visits during siesta hours were strictly tabu. At four most of the men and women went to the nine-hole golf-course. . . . My relations with the British officials were strained until I adapted myself to their three primary social interests, which were golf, hunting, and the sundowner circuit. . . . At a sundowner the quiet officiousness of the British was replaced by talkative friendliness.

The early colonial period in Nigeria reveals trends in expatriate society that became solidified during the Classic Period of Colonialism, the interwar era. A discussion of that era is well beyond the scope of this paper. Those interested, however, might study the problems faced by the Church of the Brethren in establishing missions in the Bura area in the 1920s (Edinburgh House, Box 271).

Northern Nigeria provided the prototype for indirect rule, a situation that originally developed from necessity as an *ad hoc* set of social relationships and then became transformed into a quasi-sacred cultural set of principles. These principles determined when, where, how, and with whom interactions could take place. Furthermore, Northern Nigeria had the reputation for being the locus of the best overseas administrators, and, therefore, of being another type of model. Finally, Northern Nigeria was not a settler colony. The number of expatriates was always small and the categories to which each expatriate belonged clearly delineated.

The British established colonial government in a sparsely settled area containing numerous minority ethnic groups. To govern this area they had few officers, fewer of whom were well trained. They quickly formed an alliance with the ruling Fulani, whose views regarding political, social, and economic reality it was convenient to accept. Within the British ruling group there were people who threatened the fundamental perception of reality that justified Indirect Rule. While each group that differed from the dominant section of the British segment did so for different and at times antagonistic reasons, each shared the fact of support from the metropolitan area and could not simply be crushed or ignored.

Each category had its own reasons for being in Nigeria but all were subordinate to the cause of empire, for quite clearly no expatriate could be in Nigeria without the permission of the government. Therefore, while there were conflicts within the expatriate community, there were no disagreements regarding British right to rule. For example, while Miller quite openly argued that the cross should follow the sword, he never objected to the right of the sword to be where it was. Although the specifics of the operation of government might be questioned, the right to govern never was.

These arguments, however, were not quibbles. They were real conflicts, ones which determined patterns of interaction. Missionaries tended to view the Fulani as "the enemy," frequently failing to distinguish between ruling and cattle Fulani, while tending to idealize the Hausa. The British officers did the opposite. The examples given above illustrate both "type" errors. The Hausa-Fulani alliances or the intricacies of the *jihad* tended to be victims of ideological bias. Quite expectedly, the ruling elite of the British and local authorities increasingly identified their causes, and missionaries tended to identify with non-Fulani and non-Muslims.

Within the expatriate community arguments, regarding means could be carried outside Northern Nigeria. Examples are given that clearly show that appeals to the governor could succeed. At the same time, one could always appeal to London. The final success of the Church of the Brethren provides a dear example of the impact metropolitan politics could have on policy in the north. Furthermore, there were conflicts within each segment of expatriate society. The administrative services were no more monolithic than were the missionaries. Again, while each presented a unified front toward other segments, and all did so toward Nigerians, each was internally differentiated. To those familiar with the work of Evans-Pritchard (1940), Gluckman (1954), or Durkheim and Mauss (1963), this fact will not appear strange. To many analysts, however, plural societies have been treated as rather static entities whose members from constituent parts met in stereotypical encounters.

What is being suggested is that a more dynamic perspective will prove useful. Specifically, conflict within each segment demands analysis and is as problematic as agreement. Over what issues will there be splits within each constituent of each of the plural segments? Over which issue will there be agreements? The use of the, Mahdi as a bogeyman illustrates the use of appeal to 'a common enemy to compel unity in the face of opposition. At root plural societies last because members of the ruling segment agree to confine their disagreements within the plural framework.

They also last because alliances are formed across segments. The administration formed alliances with the old ruling elite, thereby changing a system under the guise of preserving it. These alliances and those of the missionaries with enemies of the system were the results of differential perceptions of reality, within and between each segment. A host of problems in this area has only begun to be explored.

In addition, the entire issue of ties to the metropolitan areas and the outside world demand as much attention as those of differential perceptions and patterns of interaction. This paper has not explored that issue. Certainly, however, it has suggested that these ties were of vital importance to events within Nigeria. Appeals to those outside the north were frequent. Now it is vital to work out a typology of appeals, frequency, and success of each. Van den Bergh's (1973) insight, based on his research at the University of Ibadan, that conflict within an elite segment is confined within reasonable limits and works to preserve the system because of basic agreement on ultimate organizational goals, including its preservation, holds true for the colonial situation. Nevertheless, no one has taken the next logical step and described and analyzed the significant issue of the unexpected consequences of the struggle.

Chapter Four

Indirect Rule—The Hausa of Nigeria: The Nigerian Example

British colonial policies such as military force, anti-slavery legislation, taxes, Commodification, and indirect rule all combined to change Northern Nigeria's rural social formation. For slave owners, who made up a growing part of Northern Nigeria's social formation before colonial rule and who used slave labor on plantations, mining, leather works and textile production, the nature of transformation was two-fold. First, British colonial rule weakened the economic conditions of slave owners. Second, after weakening their economic base, British colonial rule transformed these slave owners into various class and non-class positions. The paper concludes that the transformation of former slave owners into these new class and non-class positions negatively affected their ability to accumulate wealth as they previously had. Therefore, they found it difficult to transform themselves to feudalists or capitalists. Colonial rule reduced them to positions of traders and administrators. In these positions they could not participate in productive economic activities until the end of colonial rule. (Ferdnance 1998, 233)

It is essential to keep in mind that the expatriate community was absolutely and relatively small. In 1931, for example, there were 1825 expatriates in Northern Nigeria in a total population of 11, 434, 924, or .01595% of the population. This meant that there were .0069958 non-Nigerians per square mile compared with about 41 Nigerians (See Brooke 1931). It is no wonder that Kirke-Green refers to colonial officers as "the thin white line (ms)."

The presence of Islam among the Fulani and other northern peoples also helped define the overall situation. At the time of colonial rule, Islam was essentially a colonial religion. It had not yet seeped down to the common people. In truth, moreover, the rapid spread of Islam in the Hausa-Fulani area, from about 5% of the population to about 80% of it is a result of deliberate British colonial policy. Quite simple, the British did not possess the means to rule the vast area of Northern Nigeria directly. Consequently, they found it convenient to encourage the appeal of Islam and to rule through Muslim rulers "indirectly." The end result of Indirect Rule was the strengthening of a foreign group of conquerors, the Fulani, and the acceptance of their idealized version of political reality. It was, needless to say, a version which local people, including the Hausa, rejected.

In addition, however, to being useful, the Fulani version of political reality coincided with the British ideology of Indirect Rule. In sum, the Fulani claimed to come from Arabia and to form an aristocratic Islamic elite of scholars. When the Hausa rulers failed in their duty to uphold proper Islamic principles, they, under the leadership of Shehu Usman dan Fodio, waged a jihad and established a true Islamic state. That state, the Sokoto Caliphate, united a number of subordinate states under its rule in what had been the Hausa area of the North, plus other areas never under their rule. Thus, from 1804 until the British conquest of 1903, the Fulani reigned supreme in Northern Nigeria and their governmental structure was essentially that of a "purified" Hausa state (see Hendrixson 1980, Dorward 1974, and Smith 1960).

British colonial officers did not allow the facts to cloud their visions. They were armed with the evolutionary anthropology of their day and used its tenets where convenient to get on with the tasks of governing. That task of governing included the "pacification" of Northern Nigeria. In this task the Fulani version of reality suited their fancy and needs. British fancy posited people at various stages of development. So-called Hamitic peoples, presumably were more advanced than various "Negroid" peoples, and Muslims were obviously closer to Christians than "pagans." Fulani claims to non-Negroid ancestry and their adherence to Islam allowed the British to categorize them as "true rulers" and natural allies of the British. (See Evans-Pritchard 1951 for a succinct summary of the prevalent ideology. Lugard 1906, 1919, and 1922 offer sources of his views on the Fulani.)

This British ideology had very real implications for the development of Fulani ethnicity. Interestingly, as Henrixson (1980: 56) indicates "Prior to the beginning of the jihad in 1804, the category Fulani was not politically important for the Toronkawa," that branch of the Fulfulde speaking people who were in Nigeria. The Toronkawa, significantly, did not consider themselves Fulani. However, between 1804 and the British conquest of Sokoto the Toronkawa arrogated to themselves as a ruling elite and to those pastoralists who supported them the term "Fulani" (Henrixson 1980: 45). Moreover, the British further consolidated the Fulani claims to provide a natural ruling aristocracy and to make that a current hallmark of their ethnic identity.

The Hausa-Fulani became models of civilization. The British, in fact, raised them above models. They made them partners in the spreading of high culture to the pagans. Those "pagans" who resisted British rule became "truculent" and "cannibals" in the literature (Dorward 1974: 459-60). Consequently, the spread of the Hamitic/ Hausa-Fulani culture, including Islam was a positive stage in promoting cultural-evolutionary progress. It is not surprising, therefore, that in order to validate their hold on their favored position; Fulani began to stress tradition, defined in terms of religion, as an ethnic boundary marker in this period (Henrixson 1980: 57). In fact, as Crowder (1964 In Markovitz 1971: 28) states

> . . . in the earliest interwar period many emirs and chiefs ruled as "sole native authorities," a position which gave them for practical purposes more power than they had in precolonial days, where they were either subject to control by a council or liable to deposition if they became too unpopular. . . . There was thus a minimal undermining of the traditional sources of authority. The main change for the Fulani Emirs of Northern Nigeria, for instance, was that they now owed allegiance to the British Government rather than to the Sultan of Sokoto. . . .

Dorward agrees that Indirect Rule in Northern Nigeria provided the model for the rest of British rule in Africa and that it frequently increased the power of traditional rulers. Moreover, many of these "traditional" rulers were of rather recent origin. Dorward maintains that local rulers were active agents in strengthening their own power and hoodwinked political officers who were frequently willing dupes in the social construction of reality. The Fulani were masters of this particular colonial game and they cooperated with the British in the negotiation of Fulani ethnicity in Northern Nigeria.

There were, however, people within the British expatriate group who threatened the fundamental perception of reality that justified indirect rule and the negotiated definition of Fulani ethnicity. Among those who posed the greatest threat were missionaries. Missionaries had their own version of reality, one that did not view the Muslim Fulani as the natural rulers or Islam as a stage that would enhance so-called pagans. Colonial officers feared that missionary activity would rupture their tenuous alliance with Fulani rulers.

To bolster their own power British administrators created the "official wisdom," that emirs opposed not only Christian missionaries but also Western education. In fact, some, but not all emirs opposed the fact that missionaries were the primary carriers of Western education to the North. Ubah (1976: 352) and Omatseye (1981) argue that emirs based their opposition to Western education on the seemingly inextricable link between it and missionaries. Ubah (1976: 363) is even of the opinion that the emirs would not have strongly resisted mission schools if colonial pressure had been brought to bear. He states "but the administration itself was timid, and the emirs did not hesitate to exploit this timidity." In fact, British opposition to missionaries in Islamic areas was far from timid and suggests that it was their perception of the North as Islamic that led them to keep missionaries out of the area for so long. That perception, moreover, was essential to the ideology that supported what Dorward (1974) terms the "working misunderstanding." The fact that missionaries in general actively opposed the façade of indirect rule did not find them many supporters in the Northern Nigerian administration.

It is relevant to recall that the sacred tenets of Indirect Rule required local financial support for all local governmental functions, including education. Since Western education was too expensive for local support and since missionaries were the only other feasible alternative for Western education, then the second tenet of Indirect Rule came into play, the presumed innate hostility between Islam and Christianity, and the definition of the North as Islamic except for the Middle Belt area, the area around the confluence of the Niger and Benue Rivers. The inherent logic of indirect rule demanded that missionaries be opposed even when they were the only feasible vehicles for education (Graham 1966:167-68). Abernathy (1971) and Pushkin (1971) have graphically discussed the disruptive effects of differential educational policies. In sum, even in "progressive" emirates the North was woefully behind the Southern part of Nigeria in every field of modern education. It's system of education was run by Southerners and expatriates.

It appears clear, then, that the Fulani or "Hausa-Fulani" as the British began to refer to the ruling elite of the old Hausa emirates, had to redefine their identity in light of the new political situation that the British conquest brought to Northern Nigeria, indeed to Nigeria as a whole. The very uses of religious and traditional criteria as an ethnic device, as Henrixson (1980) so nicely notes, is best understood as a response to their negotiations with the British and a means toward establishing themselves as "natural rulers" in the colonial evolutionary ideology. Their alliance with Hausa people has parallels elsewhere in Northern Nigeria in the alliance of "Hausa" peoples with those whom they have conquered in a strategy with a double purpose: to validate their claims to legitimacy and to recruit allies in that cause (Salamone 1973, 1975a, 1975b, 1980, 1982, and Salamone and Swanson 1979). The only difference is that they have hyphenated their new ethnic identity, Fulani, with that of the Hausa, in an effort to keep their alliance with the pastoral Fulani and to safeguard their claims to legitimacy as heirs and purifiers of the old Hausa tradition.

The response locked the Hausa-Fulani rulers into certain behaviors. They had to acquiesce in matters impinging on the ideological and economic essence of Indirect Rule. Thus, "real" Muslim emirs opposed missionaries and modern education. Local authorities had to collect taxes for British officials even in cases where there were no legitimate traditional bases for such actions. Although the Hausa-Fulani rulers received very real political benefits for their compliance in these transactions, there were also very real costs; namely, the resulting backwardness of the North in comparison with the rest of Nigeria and the reactionary requisites of being a Hausa-Fulani emir. Islam, which has often been a true modernizing agent, as for example under the Aga Khans, became a roadblock in Nigeria's development.

Conclusion

Throughout the colonial world colonial powers created situations that led to the emergence of new or newly defined ethnic groups. People reacted to the exigencies of the colonial situation through forming groups that protected their situations or that enabled them to seek a better position in the novel reality of colonial political, social, economic, and religious life. The Zulu and Sotho, for example, materialized from the conditions of British colonialism in South Africa. The Yoruba, a collection of warring and disparate peoples speaking related languages and sharing core traditions, found it expedient to shape a common identity to interact with other similar created identities in the colonial situation of Nigeria.

Ethnic identities are after all situational, as Ronald Cohen (1978: 388) has argued. "Ethnicity is first and foremost situational . . . the interactive situation is a major determinant of the level of inclusiveness employed in labeling self and others." What Cohen states about ethnic identity is also true of other identities as well. Moreover, it is through interaction and symbols that shape the content and perception of interaction that identities are formed, established, and maintained.

A brief look at Goffman's view of how one establishes social identity helps clarify the issue. Social identity is closely allied to what he termed the "front" or "front stage." The front is "that part of the individual's performance which regularly functions in a general and fixed fashion to define the situation for those who observe the performance" (Goffman 1949, p. 22). The front has a "collective representation" and sets up an appropriate "setting," "appearance," and "manner" for the performance of the social role, such as regional identity, which the actor is performing. For consistency of interaction, the social actor must fill the role and communicate its meaning in a coherent manner.

It is here that Goffman discusses impression management, which is the way in which a social actor controls and communicates information via his or her performance. Because the actor is coherently playing a role, he or she becomes that role for the duration of the performance. Other social actors can fine tune their reactions accordingly. This dramatic realization is clearly seen in the performance of identity in colonial multiethnic situations.

Goffman indicates that social actors make a greater effort to perform an idealized version of the role through being more consistent in adhering to norms, mores, and laws of society than when alone. The audience has a great deal to do with consistency of performance. In other words, the other everywhere helps shape the performance of people. The performer hides inconsistent beliefs and everyday behavior that does not conform with expectations while choosing to emphasize behavior consonant with the idealized image of the role.

But we can go beyond this profoundly simple fact. Social actors, no matter how cynical, like stage actors often inhabit their roles so completely that they become that role. We find people seeking to distinguish themselves, that is their real selves, from their fronts or social selves. They may bring family pictures to work or play music they particularly like there, even if it is not what others may like. Whatever the means, there is an attempt to fight the capture of their innermost selves from their social fronts. But often anyway the two may merge. Perhaps, one has become so socialized that there is little difference between the two. Or there may be great reward in being thought one with pioneers whom people admire. The feedback process has a great deal to do with the overall process of identity formation and identification.

The colonial authority had culturally mummified "tradition" via historical acts of promulgation. Abner Cohen (1993), however, has drawn attention to another aspect that is more subversive. His work has been concerned with the powerful forces of culture, through music and dance performance, in mobilizing a popular awareness of underlying political and economic interests. In elaborating this theme in the present chapter, I wish to consider the extent to which the ebb and flow of tides of the popular expectation generated through dancing have a cosmic dimension.

Such performances may be considered as collective representations in a Durkheimian sense. They express and promote the growth of a certain confidence, a mutual credibility; a gathering will to succeed that is as relevant to understanding subversive popular movements as it is to understanding the dynamics of the market in the mainstream domain of economics. Cohen demonstrates how a group may reconstitute itself on different bases, how new identities are fore fronted to maintain cohesion, and how this new focus can become a basis for mobilization and transformation of the community. In his analysis of the Hausa community of Sabo, he argues cogently that the group reestablished its solidarity through its recognition of and adherence to a particular form of Islam, as the reference to ethnic solidarity became increasingly less viable.

Ethnic identity is a type of political identity. It is a means of mobilizing support to attain perceived goals, support which calls upon the principle of ethnicity, or presumed common descent (R. Cohen 1978). That it changes over time to suit various situations has been established in numerous places (Hendrixson 1980).

Although ethnic, and therefore, political identities are mutually negotiated, there are limits to the process. The British, for instance, possessed a colonial ideology based on evolutionary anthropology. That ideology was indeed, flexible but it was not totally malleable. When it could not be reinterpreted or adjusted, it forced rigid, even logical, compliance within the constructed boundaries of the defined realities. This compliance and Hausa-Fulani performance of their colonial influenced identity during the enactment of the colonial drama helped fix that identity during the postcolonial era and the ethnic conflicts of that period, a process we see reenacted within the boundaries of the former Soviet Union (Marker 2004).

"During these periods of expansion, Western European and Soviet powers formed new colonial multiethnic provinces (e.g., Rhodesia, French Indonesia, German East Africa) and satellite states (e.g., Czechoslovakia, Yugoslavia). They did so with little regard for the people living in the newly controlled areas, or for existing geographic or cultural boundaries. Populations that had previously identified themselves as distinct, based on their cultural, ethnic, and/or religious heritage, were forced to unify under a single national identity. The new multiethnic colonial territories and Soviet states were maintained, upheld, and controlled through the use of violence, and through the implementation of imperialist policies. Certain populations were denied their political, economic, social, and human rights. Imperialist policies promoted ethnic rivalry by favoring one group above the others, distributed resources in an unequal manner, disallowed democratic governments, and prohibited local participation in governmental decisions and actions (Marker 2004)."

Once the superior power of the colonial power was removed, the disparate ethnic groups began to struggle, often gruesomely, among themselves for the control of what the colonial powers had left. Too often genocidal struggles and outright greed marred the gains of the struggle for freedom from colonial oppression. Despite the frequent setbacks, however, there have been historic gains in places like South Africa and Ghana, for example, to find ways to overcome the identity politics fostered under colonial regimes. New realities can foster more productive group interaction than those promoted in the divide and rule politics of colonialism and neocolonialism. It is important that policies be developed in African states and throughout the world to encourage realities that help promote these benevolent new realities.

Chapter Five

Overview of the Lucy Memorial Freed Slaves' Home

The abolition of the slave trade and slavery was prominent among British rationalizations for their conquest and control of what came to be known as the Protectorate of Northern Nigeria. The Slavery Proclamation of 1901 abolished the legal status of slavery, proclaimed all children born after April 1, 1901, free, and made it illegal to return fugitive slaves (Northern Nigeria Colonial Report No. 346 1900/1901: 15). As Lovejoy and Hogendorn (1993) note that once in power British enthusiasm for the immediate and quick abolition of slavery cooled under the pressure of on the ground realities, primarily the need to rule the newly acquired territory cheaply through the cooperation of the newly conquered slave trading rulers of the Northern Emirates. Lord Lugard's policy of the dual mandate, or indirect rule, has been discussed in detail in numerous works but its relationship to the establishment of Freed Slaves' Homes has been relatively neglected.

In actuality, Freed Slaves' Homes were an integral part of the strategy that Lugard and his successors employed to abolish the slave trade while discouraging runaway slaves (Lovejoy and Hogendorn [1993: 83-84, 96-97, 122-123]). These homes were established to train young slaves freed from slave traders and whose place of origin was generally unknown. Basically, these institutions were technical training schools for young children, not refuges for runaway slaves. Through keeping adults from gaining admittance and refuge in these homes, the colonial power avoided supporting an institution that would entice people to flee their owners. At the same time it could claim to be aiding homeless children freed from the evils of slavery. Moreover, these children generally had been taken at such an early age that it was impossible to trace their origins. Through providing training in useful skills the Home ensured that they would not become a burden on society while also securing their loyalty to the British raj.

Origins of the Freed Slaves' Homes in Nigeria

It is clear that Lugard's real aim in establishing Freed Slaves' Homes at Lokoja, Zungerua, and Bornu was to prevent escaped slaves from having a refuge while providing a training school for young children, for whom Lugard did have a real concern. Young boys were to be trained in useful skills and were regarded as government apprentices. Young girls were to be trained in such a manner as to be able to contract good marriages. Lovejoy and Hogendorn (1993: 83) indicate that the children were regarded as government slaves.

There is no doubt that there was a serious problem regarding enslaved children in Northern Nigeria. Despite Lugard's 1901 proclamation abolishing slavery, enslavement not only continued but grew during the period of 1900 to 1920. Moreover, it took a particularly ugly turn. According to Olusanya (1966: 524)

> . . . emphasis was laid on the buying and selling of children instead of adults. This was because the slave traders were now aware that the trade was a contraband one and adults would easily escape their clutches and report them to the District Officers. For instance, more infants were purchased for Eastern Muri, Yola and German Adamawa and conveyed to Bassa by canoe at night, where they were bought by the Okpoto for resale in Southern Nigeria.

According to Olusanya, the Nupe were the greatest slave traders of the time, and they gave children whom they enslaved Nupe facial marks in order to prevent detection.

Upon freeing these slaves, the administration was faced with a dilemma. Many children did not know their origins and so could not be returned to their home villages. Those children who did know their home villages often came from areas that were so poor that their parents had originally sold them into slavery. At first, the government placed children with foster parents as wards. However, this proved little if at all better than slavery. The children were badly used. Therefore, the government began to apprentice boys to Public Works Department and found jobs for girls as servants. Some children were given to missionaries for training. Women were found husbands but many eventually were driven into prostitution. Moreover, as the number of liberated slaves, mainly children, increased, the government had to find another solution.

The Freed Slaves' Homes emerged, therefore, as a response to the problem. Lugard, however, was always suspicious of their long-term usefulness, for he did not like involving missionaries overmuch in the government's affairs, fearful that such involvement would antagonize the Muslim powers. Additionally, he was concerned that these homes would encourage fugitive slaves to roam the countryside. Consequently, he used a vagrancy ordinance to counteract his own law against returning fugitive slaves to their former owners (see Lovejoy and Hogendorn 1993: 96-96, 122-123). Therefore, Lugard allowed Freed Slaves' Homes to exist only for children and under the strictest government supervision.

So strict were Lugard's terms, in fact, that the first attempt to establish Freed Slaves' Homes in Lokoja, one for men and one for women, fell through. Lokoja's Resident, W. S. Sharpe, negotiated an agreement with the C.M.S.' Acting Secretary at Lokoja to administer the two homes. Lugard, however, insisted on adding terms to the agreement that caused the C.M.S. to withdraw their support. They saw no reason to concern themselves with the tender feelings of "the Mohammedan master who considers himself robbed of his property," as Lugard termed the former slaveholder (Lugard, Jebba, C.O. 446/10 No. 23453, 16/6/1900). Nor will they willing to substitute Lugard's "moral instruction" for their teaching of Christianity to the youngsters. Neither would they submit all personnel changes to his prior approval. Finally, they would not agree to Lugard's desire that they cease preaching equality of races. Lugard was clear in his opposition to such activity as his 1905-1906 Parliamentary Report makes clear.

> I am informed that they preach the equality of Europeans and natives, which, however true from a doctrinal point of view, is apt to be misapplied by people in a low state of development, and interpreted as an abolition of class distinction. (Parliament Paper 1907. LIV Report on Northern Nigeria for 1905-1906)

With typical rigor and determination, Lugard decided to establish a Freed Slaves' Home along his own lines, based on considerations of similar homes in Africa (Colonial Report No. 346 for 1900-1901 and

Rouche 1950). The first Freed Slaves' Home was officially dedicated on January 1, 1904, in Zungeru, although it had actually opened in October 1903. In February of the same year Lugard opened another Home in Maifonni, Bornu, to accommodate freed slaves from Adamawa, including the German section. Lugard was concerned about having these children make a journey of over 1,000 miles to Zungeru.

A census of its first occupants gives a clear impression of Lugard's overriding philosophy regarding the purpose of the Homes. The Zungeru Home had 184 charges, 65 adults and 129 children. These freed slaves were under the supervision of a Lady Supervisor and her African workers. In the Bornu Home there were, according to Olusanya, 142 people; 11 of these people were adult women, 19 were young ladies aged 12-20, and the remaining 112 were under 11 years old. The homes were to care for children and unmarried women, in hopes of finding useful jobs for the males and suitable husbands for the women.

An interesting adjunct to the Bornu Home was Liberty Farm, a settlement for those freed slaves deemed unfit for the Home, either because of age or disposition. These ex-slaves were also deemed not competent to be allowed to make their own way in Nigeria. There were a number of reasons for so judging them, unfamiliarity with the language, age, disabilities, or personal character, for example. Lugard, however, felt some responsibility for them. At first 6 shillings per week were set aside for food but that was later reduced to 12 shillings per month. In conformity with the overall concept of indirect rule, the government hoped that the village would become self-sufficient, enabling it to end the Home and place youngsters in foster care with adults, a hope that never was realized (Kirk-Greene 1958).

The Zungeru and Bornu Homes put into operation a number of Lugard's basic principles. A government committee, consisting of a number of senior officials, including the District magistrate, oversaw the general administration of the Homes. In conformity with Lugard's desire to see local institutions self-supporting, or at least not making application for funds outside Nigeria, the Homes were aided by charitable donations from two agencies; Lugard was a trustee of one of the charities, the Rebecca Hussey Charity. The other charity was the St. Giles Trust. In addition, the Home earned money through its work as well as receiving bride price for women living in the Home.

Lugard's Philosophy Regarding the Homes

The day-to-day operation of the Homes was also in keeping with Lugard's general philosophy. Strict discipline enforced a rigorous orderly routine. The inmates rose early and worked late, with breaks for meals and recreation. Punishment was ferocious and bordered on abuse. Children were routinely given cuts on the head for misbehavior. It was not unusual for boys and girls to be locked up for days on short rations for relatively minor offenses.

Education suffered in the Home because of the Government's concern that the Home pay its own way. Children were often apprenticed out to various Government Departments as laborers or artisans to learn a trade. Some wards were sent to other African colonies. It is true that, because of previous sad experiences, the Government took precautions for the safety and well-being of their wards, inspecting conditions or requiring other that the Governments of other British colonies do so on their behalf when children were assigned as wards to other West African British colonies. Eventually and inevitably, many of the children became wards of missionaries, some of the youngsters even went to England as wards of various people.

These youngsters generally did quite well for themselves, better on the average than those who remained wards of the Government. The schools taught the basics of reading, writing, and arithmetic and how to work. Specifically, they taught some crafts—tailoring, carpentry, and drilling—and other domestic skills—laundering, baking, and gardening. Since there was a lack of trained teachers, the schools used a system through which the more advanced students taught the less advanced ones.

Sir Percy Girouard, High Commissioner for Nigeria, appointed a Committee to investigate the feasibility of the Government's continuing to operate the Freed Slaves' Homes. Girouard charged the committee to ascertain whether the Homes fulfilled their goals of effectively and efficiently preparing liberated slaves who were children for useful lives, to sample public opinion of the Homes, and to determine whether alternative means for the preparation of these children could be found that would better serve the needs of the Government and population (Report on a Committee appointed by the Order of His Excellency Sir Percy Girouard, High Commissioner, Northern Nigeria, to investigate matters connected with the Freed Slaves' Home in Secretariat Minute Paper No. 5091/ 1907).

The Committee Report was a negative one, faulting the Homes on training their charges appropriately for self-reliance in any definition of the term. It is true that the members of the Committee had never viewed Government operation of the Homes in a kindly manner. It is also true that they based their judgment of the Homes' success at preparing its residents for Nigerian society on a stagnant view of that society. Nevertheless, they also considered that the most successful members of the Homes were sent to missionaries as wards. Therefore, it might be better to have a missionary body assume responsibility for administration of the liberated children. Accordingly, the Committee recommended that the care of the Homes' charges should be turned over to a missionary body. It went further and began to prepare for such a handing over.

The Sudan United Mission and the Freed Slaves' Home Movement

In fact, advances had been made even before the Committee met. In 1904, for example, the Deputy High Commissioner requested the Sudan United Mission (SUM) to take over the running of the Freed Slaves' Homes. Similarly, in the same year the Resident of Muri Division, Popham Lobb, requested the SUM to open a Freed Slaves' Home there in union with an industrial village the administration was considering. The institution would allow the repatriation of exported slave children. When, as a result of the work of the Committee, the Government again approached the SUM to open a Freed Slave Home, it accepted.

There were a number of reasons why the SUM accepted the responsibility for founding and running a Freed Slaves' Home. In an article in the *Lightbearer* Kumm presents reasons for accepting the government's offer. He states that in August, 1904, the Deputy High Commissioner for Northern Nigeria, ask him whether there would be any interest in the SUM to establish a Freed Slaves' Home in Northern Nigeria. The next year, on May 9, a Mr. R. Poham Lobb wrote Kumm exploring the establishment of a farm colony for adult slaves whom the Government had freed. Private sources also urged the SUM to get involved in a Freed Slaves' Home. A R. M. Rankiz of Glasgow promised a large sum of money on behalf of Dalcairn, Pollokshields if it did. The British Resident of Muri Province, Captain Ruxton, suggested that the SUM open a new station in Dien. Lugard, the High Commissioner, approved the suggestion. Dien was the area of Northern Nigeria with the most Freed

Slaves, from which the new Home would draw its clientele The adults were to be instructed in European style agriculture and sent out to teach these techniques to their people.

Kumm continued to state some deeper reasons for establishing the Home in conformity with the evangelical nature of the SUM.

> As religious teaching would form one of the main features of the proposed Memorial Home, the liberated slaves on their return would become, we may hope, evangelists to their own people. Friends in different parts of England have suggested a Memorial to the late Mrs. Kumm. Mrs. Kumm's last book, *Our Slave State*, though not directly written for the Sudan, contains many thoughts which show that the poor, dark, homeless, parentless little ones of Africa were continually in her mind.

There were a number of other important people, such as the Earl of Elgin, who urged the SUM to open a Freed Slaves' Home. There were also members of the rank and file who wanted such an establishment. There was general agreement among the supporters of Lucy Guinness Kumm that such a Home was a fitting memorial for all her work.

Thus, the SUM accepted Government offers for a number of reasons but mainly because it was planning to open a Freed Slaves' Home in Northern Nigeria in honor of Dr. Karl Kumm's deceased wife, Lucy Guinness Kumm. In October 1906, the SUM had, in fact applied to the Secretary of State for the Colonies to open the Lucy Memorial Freed Slaves' Home. The SUM received official permission in November to begin its operation. It was not until 1908, however, that plans were completed for transfer of the Homes' residents to the new facility (Secretariat Minute Paper 4059/1906; Maxwell n.d: 77).

In addition, at Dr. Kumm's suggestion, a very effective Ladies' Committee was formed, the object of which was threefold: (1) Prayer for the Mission work in the Suda, (2) Spreading news about this work and getting others interested in the work, and (3) Collecting subscriptions from South Africans for the support of missionaries.

Subsequent reports make it clear that the Ladies' Committee was quite effective. The committee grew in membership each year, accepted African women into their fieldwork, and gave an increasing amount of money and service to evangelical work, and conducted a successful drive to include schoolchildren in a foster parent subscription program in support of the freed slave children taken in the Lucy Memorial Home. Her impact on the SUM, including the establishment of the Lucy Memorial Freed Slaves' Home, is evidenced by the following:

> The formation of the Sudan United Mission will ever be associated with the burning missionary zeal and consecrated life of the late Mrs. Karl Kumm, the last years of whose life were devoted to the organization of an effort to carry the Gospel to the Sudan. . . . After careful and prayerful consideration, it was unanimously decided to found a Freed Slaves' Home as a lasting memorial to her life and work. (The Lucy Memorial Freed Slaves' Home: 3)

Therefore, it is not surprising that in his "The Open Sore of Africa: Slave Raiding," Kumm (915-916) writes in tribute to his wife who had died in 1906 in Northfield, Massachusetts, while on a fund-raising trip

> (W)hat more fitting memorial to the life of the late Mrs. Kumm could be devised than a home for those rescued from the awful fate of slavery—a home where Christian love would reign, and the Gospel of redeeming grace be taught, a home where lives shall be delivered from sin and suffering and be transformed into sanctified, consecrated service to Christ.

SUM members perceived Lucy's death as a martyrdom. She had gone to the United States on a fund raising mission. Because of that trip and her desire to complete her latest manuscript, a 100 page tract on the hardships of the Congo people, she postponed essential abdominal surgery against her doctor's advice. On August 6, 1906, she finished her book and entered the hospital. She had postponed her operation too long and died on August 12. Her death spurred the SUM to establish its Freed Slaves' Home in her honor, using her example as a rallying point.

If the founding of the Home was a result of the influence of Lucy Guinness Kumm, its actual operation was an attempt to put those principles into operation. The Home provided a rallying point for the SUM's crusade against the slave trade, which according to Lugard himself (1907, reprinted in The Lucy Memorial Freed Slaves' Home: 6-7) noted that "There is a very active slave trade through Bornu, hundred of slaves being brought into the markets of Dikwa and Mandara, and conveyed across British Bornu for sale at Kabi." Lugard indicated that he was taking strong action to end the trade. However, despite strong efforts, including overcrowding the Freed Slaves' Home in Bornu and founding

Liberty Village, the trade is so lucrative that it continues to grow. Moreover, Lugard warns that the caravans routes, forced to avoid detection, travel only under the cover of darkness and took bush roads. He complains that the "slaves freed are chiefly the very lowest type of cannibals." Later, he notes that the terrible famine caused families to sell their children. He recounts the case of slave traders cornered who took their canoe to midstream and purposely capsized it, leading to the drowning of twelve of the twenty-two children in the canoe.

Kumm (1907: 128-129), himself, describes these canoes in a chilling passage:

> On the Upper Benue last year, we saw again and again canoes full of what must have been slave children that were being transported down the river. The Government officials liberated quite a number of them, and it was suggested that the missionaries should start a Freed Slaves' Home, to train these children into useful men and women and to teach them the things of God.

> At Government headquarters in Northern Nigeria, at Zungeru, there is already a freed slaves' home. When I spoke to the resident doctor there, he told me that the children are usually in such a dreadful state of neglect that about 5% of them die within a short time of their arrival at headquarters. If with all the care that the white man can give these children 5% of them die after they are liberated, how many must die when in the hands of the cruel, selfish native traders.

Lucy Guinness Kumm worked for the establishment of the Home to aid children freed from the slave trade and to ensure that they would not find themselves returned to it. The very presence of slave homes, she believed, would serve as a model for a better life, provide a sanctuary for freed children and adult females, and a base from which missionaries could sally forth to combat the trade itself. Kumm (The Lucy Memorial Freed Slaves' Home: 10) addresses the issue directly.

> Mohammedanism, with its avowed acceptance, practice, and teaching of slavery, is, on that account alone, one of the most wicked, if not the most wicked religion on the face of God's earth. Martin Luther was not far wrong when he called Mahomet "the first-born son of Satan."

The Home would be a fitting tribute to his wife and, he implies, but an important first step to greater battle with the Muslims.

The resolution establishing the Home clearly demonstrates this interest as well as Lucy Guinness Kumm's influence on the philosophy of the Home. One section, in particular, outlines the mission of the Home as its founders conceived it. Section 4 states that the Resident of Muri Province, Captain Ruxton, invited the SUM to establish a missionary station in Djen. Djen bordered Yola and Muri Provinces. Moreover, most of the slaves taken in Northern Nigeria were coming from the area, leading to serious depopulation. The Government hoped that a Freed Slaves' Home would provide instruction in agriculture and European technology. Upon repatriation to their homelands, these liberated slaves would spread the knowledge they had gained.

It was an idea that the SUM greatly favored and included to incorporate additional ideas. "As religious teaching would form one of the main features of the proposed Memorial Home, the liberated slaves on their return would become, we may hope evangelists to their own people." The Home would clearly teach Christianity. Lugard's reluctance to having missionaries conduct the Freed Slaves' Homes had been overcome, or at least circumvented, as the exigencies of economics began to weigh heavily on the Administration.

Establishing the Home

Negotiation appeared to drag on for some time. However, both the mission and the government desired the Home and in due time an agreement was reached. The daily operations of the school followed the subsequent pattern.

On 2nd December, 1920, the Secretary of the Sudan United Mission at Ibi received a telegram from F. M. Urling-Smith, the Director of Education, informing him that The Freed Slaves' Home was receiving a grant of £99.15.2 for its school at Wukari. A copy of the Reverend G. P. Bargery's report was enclosed along with congratulations for the state of the school. Bargery's report offers a good view of the school's operation.

The school had three European staff. These consisted of a manager, H.G. Farrant, and two teachers with English Certificates, Miss Rimmer and Miss Overy. Six Nigerian staff members are mentioned but only one appeared to be still with the school during the October 18-21 inspection, a person identified as Asa with no mention of duties or qualifications. Others are noted only as leaving on various dates with no reason given for their departures, except for Sidi who left after developing leprosy.

Bargery rated the school quite highly on its efficiency. Specifically, he noted that the children were quite clean and deported themselves well. The Staff were commended for using recreation to bring their influence to bear on the pupils.

Physical exercises basket ball, foot ball, singing and competitive games, all are thoroughly enjoyed and self control, and unselfishness kept to the fore, creating noticeable improvement in character.

Moral instruction, of course, was prominent in the school curriculum. Note that the missionaries were careful to term their religious education "moral instruction," attesting to Lugard's continuing influence on Nigerian affairs.

The school had three infant and three primary classes. There was a separate class for the blind. Bargery notes with a tinge of pride that each class was in a separate room. Records, diaries, and lessons were in good order. Bargery commends the European staff for their "time and patience with the native assistants" so that these assistants could produce such good results. A further example of Bargery's condescension and prejudice is found in his statement regarding discipline.

He commends the Staff for its improvement in correcting unnamed previous problems. Currently, he notes that there is good discipline both inside and outside the school. The community is happy. Indeed, he records that pupils regard it as a severe punishment to be kept from school attendance. The European Staff's goal of "Education by Atmosphere" reduces "tendencies to priggishness and smugness. Sneaking, a fault so common to black children, is strongly discouraged."

As Inspector, Bargery administered exams in Scripture, Reading, English, Writing, Dictation, Composition, Arithmetic, Hygiene, Geography, Drawing, Cooking and Laundry Work. In general, progress was noted in all areas. Composition was weak but it seems to be a problem, according to Bargery, in all English Schools. Scripture, not surprisingly, was a subject in which the children excelled. The children went beyond mere rote knowledge and were able to draw lessons from the material. Children did well in Reading, a course conducted in Hausa. The Practice Teachers (P.T.'s) provided valuable aid. Although the Infants were good in arithmetic, the other sections were only fair.

Bargery has an interesting commentary on Drawing that provides a charming glimpse into the school's operations.

Crayon work is good, and the walls of the school are adorned with some very creditable productions. Tablet-laying, paper cutting and folding, also latticing modeling are a great feature of the infant classes.

The children performed "practical work" daily. Girls beat floors, did the laundry, and prepared and cooked the food. Boys did farm work in the mornings. Bargery expected more supervision to be provided once the Reverend Evans arrived before the year's end. He does not elaborate on this issue and leaves it, as so many others in his report, as a hint of some interesting possibilities. He is, however, explicit enough on the generally upkeep of the School.

The School building was well-suited for its work and in generally good repair. However, there had been some unusually bad storms and the roof required rethatching. The premises easily passed sanitary inspection by the Mission's Medical Superintendent. Bargery further judged that the school's textbooks and "apparatus" were up to standards. Interestingly, he notes that the Freed Slaves' Home School was "probably the only school in Nigeria where any attempt is made to train the blind."

Crane (n.d.:21) in assessing the work of the SUM notes that in Nigeria it carried on the work of a Freed Slaves' Home and a Native Agents' Training Institution. The two institutions are linked. The Freed Slaves' Home cared for and educated freed slave children. At the time of his writing, about 1915, the Home had educated over 200 youngsters.

Crane gives a bit more information on the set up of the Home than did Bargery. He notes that the basic philosophy of education is "that the children should be trained to take their place in native life, and not become mere hangers-on of the European community." To aid the achievement of that goal, the SUM housed them in native huts rather than a European building. To encourage them to stay in "native life," the Home did not teach English at this time but rather used Hausa as the language of instruction—a practice that was obviously modified by the time of Bargery's report. The useful, or "practical" arts, were taught—farming, building, roof-making and weaving. Interestingly, Crane states that both sexes participated in these activities.

Crane also states that the aim of this enterprise was evangelization and that Christian instruction was fundamental to the entire enterprise. He does not discuss how the imparting of Christian knowledge would serve to aid young children who had already been uprooted from traditional life in better adapting to that life. In fact, his very next declaration belies that intention.

As the children grow up they are transferred to other stations where they act as the missionary's personal attendants and helpers, receiving in this way further training and education, with a view, so far as the boys are concerned, to their entering the Training Institute and becoming evangelists (Crane n.d.:20). Although girls were not considered as potential evangelists, they were sent to the Institute in order to find proper Christian husbands, providing appropriate wives for Christian evangelists. These evangelists and their devoted spouses would provide "the firm foundation of the larger Church of the future."

The SUM saw that future as one in which the African Church must be directed by Africans if it was to succeed in defeating the Muslim advance. At least at first, the African evangelists would be under European supervision. The Wukari Training Institute was thus logically connected with the Lucy Memorial Freed Slaves' Home. The basic plan of the Institute was simple enough.

Here native Christians, of whatever tribe, may be equipped for carrying the Gospel to their own people. A year in residence is followed by twelve months on an out-station to test and further develop their capabilities. They then return to the Institute for a final course (Crane n.d.:20). In keeping with their goal of preparing Africans to work in Africa, the SUM discouraged anything they thought might Europeanize these new evangelists.

The Lucy Memorial Freed Slaves' Home, thus, was part of an overall mission plan to evangelize the non-Muslim tribes of Northern Nigeria. At each SUM station there were graduates of the Home who aided in its evangelization work, including education and medical efforts. According to Crane the SUM dispensed 50,000 medical treatments and had 60,000 school attendances yearly.

Overall Aims of the SUM and the Place of the Home in those Plans

From its inception the SUM planned to make the Freed Slaves' Home a recruitment and training center for evangelists. Gibson (n.d.), for example, admitted that time was making the need for a Freed Slaves' Home less urgent. He accepted Lugard's rhetoric about slavery's abolition in Northern Nigeria. However, he quickly asserted that even though the day would come when there would be no more freed slaves to care for, the Home could be used for educational or industrial purposes. Meanwhile, there were a large number of freed slaves who urgently needed help. Gibson (n.d.:9-10) relates the story of "our Tom" to press his point. "Our Tom" was

> . . . a lad of about seventeen years of age. It is pitiable to read the story of that poor boy. Our friends brought him home, and he is now being trained for evangelistic service. He is one of the brightest boys you ever saw.

The American Branch of the Sudan United Mission's 1922 Annual Report and Review notes that the Seminary at Wukari, at the same location as the Freed Slaves' Home, is "the only CHRISTIAN school for higher education in the Sudan. Evangelistic, educational, industrial, and medical work is carried on at all the main stations of the Mission."

The Annual Report includes the "Report of the Lucy Memorial Freed Slaves' Home, Wukari, for the Year 1921." It presents an interesting sketch of overall and daily life as the Home was reaching that period Gibson had foreseen; namely, the end of caring for children who were freed slaves. The Home had 63 children, 24 boys and 33 girls, on January 1. It had 56 children on December 31. Only 1 new boy and no new girls entered the Home during the year. On the other had 6 boys and 2 girls left the Home, for an overall decrease of 7 children. 47 of these children received grants, 15 from the Southern Provinces and 32 from the Northern ones. The "new boy" was from Onitsha in the Southern Provinces. He entered on February 2.

Each of those who left was accounted for. Two died and one was married. Dates were given for all the other children who left. Thus, on August 26 one lame girl left to go to Minna; one "boy left to seek work on his own"; and one "boy left to go with missionaries to another station." On November 5 a "boy whose mandate expired on this date became a personal servant until he can find an opening to learn the printing trade." Finally, on December 1 another boy with an expired mandate left to go to a mission station. This young man was qualifying for a pupil teachership.

The Home had three European staff and three Pupil Teachers. The staff consisted of the Reverend E. Evans who was the Acting Supervisor; Miss C. E. Haigh, the matron; and Miss E. Rimmer, noted as "Teacher."

The Staff oversaw a demanding schedule for their 60 or so pupils, a schedule that included prayer, school subjects, meals, and work. The daily routine is rather clearly evoked in the timetable.

School Timetable

Rising Bell	5:30
Morning Prayers	6:30
Work	6:30-9:30
School	9:30-11:00
Meal, play and bath	11:00-2:00
Work	4:00-5:00
Meal and Play	5:00-8:00

The Closing of the Freed Slaves' Home and Evaluation of Its Work

The January 1926 *Lightbearer* had a story detailing the closing of the Freed Slaves' Home. The Home officially closed on December 31, 1925. It had served to educate and care for young freed slaves for more than seventeen years. It opened in August 1908, replacing earlier institutions, which had attempted to care for freed slaves.

As the *Lightbearer* puts it

> In the year 1908 the Government of Northern Nigeria found itself with nearly two hundred freed slave children on its hands. During the previous six or seven years the Government had been gradually bringing the country under administration, suppressing the slave raids and the slave trade, and establishing peace and order among the hundreds of war-worn and harassed peoples that had thus become members of the British Empire; and, in the course of these operations, a large body of slaves had been set free. (Dawson, p.20)

These slaves were found in various places. Some were in gangs being herded to slave markets, yoked and chained to one another. Others were for sale in markets. The British freed some from the raiders lairs, often herded into corrals like cattle. Dead bodies were frequently found along slave trails, left for carrion. Wherever found, local troops under British control freed them. Whenever possible people were restored to their home countries. If their actual homes were left, the British saw they were safely returned there. However, the raiders often destroyed people's homes.

Therefore, the British set up a number of freed slaves' villages. There was also the option of finding one's own place to live. However, it was difficult to find places for children, often far from home who had no idea of where that home might be. The British first set up a Home for these freed children in Bornu Province, then at Lokoja, finally at Zungeru. The British Colonial Government was about to place these freed children among local Muslims, a decision abhorrent to the SUM.

At this point the SUM offered to work with the government to establish a Freed Slaves' Home in which a Christian education would be provided. In their words, "Then the SUM stepped in with an offer to take the children off the Government's hands and five them a Christian upbringing; and this offer was accepted." There is a understanding that both the sacred and the secular profit in this bargain. The SUM had long wanted a Freed Slaves' Home and it planned that Home to be a Memorial to Lucy Guinness Kumm who died raising funds for the Home. In so doing, she had achieved the status of martyr. Using her name as a lure, her husband Karl Kumm found it easy to raise enough money to begin the Home.

In August 1908 about 190 children, from age 4 to 18, left Government protection to come under the care of the SUM at the Lucy Memorial Freed Slaves' Home. The SUM was aware of the terrible experiences these children had undergone. These tragedies includes seeing their parents murdered, brutalities of all kinds, kidnappings, beatings, sale into slavery, being driven miles in slave gangs, and even being sold by their own parents into slavery. And their travails did not end with their emancipation. "All, or nearly all, had traveled hundreds of miles in the various removals from one Government Home to another. And now they had another trek, to a new Home, at Rumasha, on the banks of the River Benue."

The SUM had accepted a great responsibility. In order to succeed the young and inexperienced mission had to win over the trust of the children. To do so they first had to nurse them back to health. Many of the children were disease ridden from diseases contracted during slavery. Many others were run down physically from terrible mistreatment. Unsurprisingly, the first two years were difficult ones. Some children died. Others found it difficult to respond to medical treatment. Eventually, medical treatment restored general good health.

Additionally, there was a good deal of ethnic heterogeneity among the group, making the establishment of community difficult. The children spoke different languages, had different customs, worldviews diverged and, in sum, had different cultures. The SUM refused to ignore the differences and simply treat them as English schoolchildren. Interestingly, they refused that path because it would have made the children unfit for their own society and as purveyors of Christianity. The purpose of the SUM was to mold Nigerian Christian evangelists.

> Instead of that, the ideal adopted for the children was that they should be given such an upbringing as would prepare them for living afterwards in any town or village where they might wish to settle, having learned some useful trade or occupation which would support them, and having received a Christian training, but without having been in any sense denationalized. (Dawson, p. 21)

Note the SUM was assuming that there was somehow a pan-Nigerian identity and then set its work to train people for this non-existent identity. It also decided what would be best for them educationally and religiously. An intellectual European education would denationalize them. Never mind that the education the SUM gave them helped "detribalize" them. The members of the SUM were not consciously being arrogant or colonial in their practice. However, the result was in conformity with overall racist and imperialistic British Colonial practice.

Overall, the SUM believed it had achieved its goals for the Home. The SUM had villages for the children built along the "ordinary native fashion." Their clothes were not Western but in the usual "native fashion." They taught children local handicrafts. Moreover, the children were not kept away from local life around them. However, the SUM provided a solid educational foundation and, of course, Christian instruction and values.

The SUM states almost everyone who went through the Home found it easy to settle among the surrounding people. At the same time, there was a difference between them and those who had not attended the Home. These Christian settlers stood out and the SUM expected them to bring about many converts to Christianity. Since the number of females exceeded that of males, these "surplus women" became wives for Christian converts at other SUM stations. And the SUM made sure to prepare them for marriage. They taught them weaving, farming, cooking and other important skills. The SUM sought to ensure that their former students would marry well. Indeed, many married indigenous evangelists, a situation quite pleasing to the SUM.

The SUM kept its bargain with the Government. Its school achieved high marks on the regular inspections of Government officials. Near the end of its tenure, as the SUM gained experience and confidence, the quality was so high that "It was noted by the educational authorities in Nigeria, and large grants were made for its support" (p. 22). It should be noted that there was one final move for some of the children. The Home was moved from Rumasha to Wukari because Rumasha was a center of sleeping sickness.

Overall, the Home received about two hundred fifty children. Over sixty died. About one hundred became Christians. Some found their places of origin. There was a great scattering of people. Many worked at SUM missions in one capacity or other. Some became farmers, traders, or artisans. Only a few lost touch with the Mission. Over the years, the SUM sought to maintain ties with those who had passed through the Freed Slaves' Home. Many of the missionaries of the SUM had spent some time there, especially since it was "fact" that Europeans could not stay long in West Africa for health reasons.

Certainly, the SUM was correct in feeling a sense of accomplishment in the Freed Slaves' Home. Its closing was certainly sad but it also marked a milestone in their work. About 250 children were put in their care. Many converts to Christianity came from the Home, about half of the 200 survivors. Almost all the survivors seem to have become contributing members of society. In the eyes of the SUM a number of them became not only Christians but Christian evangelists, spreading the word in the Sudan. Lucy's dream had come true. It seemed poetic justice to many: former slaves were combating Islam as evangelists.

The Home had also provided a foothold for the SUM in Nigeria and offered experience to many of its members in educational, medical, administrative and missionary work. The experience at the Home also provided techniques useful in working with government bureaucrats in other areas of Nigeria. The tacit contract which the mission had entered into opened many doors and made the SUM part of the broader expatriate colonial community.

Chapter Six

Lugard's Relations with SUM and SUM History Relevant to the Freed Slaves' Home

A number of scholars (Herskovits 1943: 394-402; Aquina 1967: 203-219; Guiart 1970: 122-138) have argued for a more processual approach to the phenomena of conversion. Such an approach stresses the active roles of the convert in responding to a proselytizing agent. Geertz (1968), for example, made the important observation that Islam is neither an independent variable nor a monolithic entity. His point is that it is idiosyncratic in every sociocultural system in which it is found and therefore cannot be used as an explanatory model in itself. Christianity has a well-developed etic code of belief and behavior that in practice allows for great variation. It is clear that the convert is not a passive recipient of a prepackaged faith, as early acculturation theory tended to suggest. Rather, the convert chooses to identify himself as a Christian or a Muslim because of emically perceived advantages. Conversion is, emically at least, a very rational process. Whether the advantages in any particular case are real is a matter for further empirical research, as I have discussed at greater length elsewhere (1972). In fact, many of the disadvantages that may accrue from conversion result just because conversion is a process and not an event; i.e., it takes place over a period of time and requires constant learning of "Christian" behavior. A convert often discovers after conversion that such behavior conflicts with internalized values or society's norms (Sahay 1968; Guiart 1970; Salamone 1972; Luzbetak 1970).

It is important to point out that Christianity is no more a monolithic entity than is Islam. It is also important to make clear that there is no "typical" convert or "typical" missionary approach, unless we are talking about stochastic relationships. Unfortunately, no one has yet supplied us with the data needed to produce these mathematical models. As a step toward gathering that data I would like to offer the following research approach and then to give an example of its application.

An important research strategy is first to discover what kind of people are learning what kind of Christianity. I grant that this should be stating the obvious, but the literature is filled with examples that prove that this is not an obvious statement (Heiss 1970: 49-53). Too often stereotypic views of missionaries replace solid empirical research. Therefore, solid analysis of the entire missionary situation and its ecological texture is sorely needed. Such an approach emphasizes conversion as a process, in fact as a number of processes, rather than as an event. It has the further advantage of working out from the individual without sacrificing the overall framework.

The Lucy Memorial Freed Slaves' Home provides an apt opportunity to examine one example of missionary endeavor over a period. It enables a close examination of the manner in which a mission organization, the Sudan United Mission (SUM), worked closely with British Administration in Nigeria. Each partner was eager to pursue its own objectives but had to do so within the parameters of existing power relationships and within the changing political scene. There was, then, a good deal of manipulation, a certain amount of agreement, and a pressing need to find means to work out disagreements.

It is necessary to take a few moments to discuss the role of the Sudan Party of missionaries in shaping Lugard's overall views. There was little patience in the missionary community for Goldie's conciliatory gestures toward Muslim rulers. In fact, European missionaries attributed much of his anti-missionary attitude to his being a Jew. Bishop Samuel Crowther, however, was not so impatient. Crowther was a Yoruba Missionary who, unfortunately, became the focal point of an attack on African agents for the Church Mission Society (CMS) by European missionaries. These attacks were led by a group of missionaries who became known as the Sudan Party.

Members of the party were in favor of "pure, simple, primitive Christianity" presented through indigenous symbols (Owoh, 1971: 279). They believed in going directly to the people over the heads of their "despotic"

Fulani rulers. To do so, they adopted the *tobe,* the traditional dress of the people, and spoke fluent Hausa. In that language they were eloquently outspoken on matters of religion, morals, and politics. Their presuppositions regarding the peaceful nature of non-Fulani and their readiness to accept Christianity added to their fervor. In fact, they believed that only the bigotry of their Fulani rulers prevented the Hausa from immediate conversion to Christianity.

They never understood that their adoption of the *tobe* caused excitement among the populace because the populace thought the missionaries were converting to Islam. Owoh (ibid.: 298) states, "The adoption of the *tobe* by European missionaries, then, was greeted with excitement by the local people because it brought the rich white missionaries within approachable distance." The failure of the members of the Sudan Party to live like Muslims, however, as well as the threat they posed to traditional Islamic teachers and the emirs created great political problems. Furthermore, the Sudan Party's opposition to African clergy had serious repercussions, with many Sierra Leonians turning on the CMS and condemning it to Hausa authorities. In addition, that policy split the northern and southern Nigerian churches for years.

Given both the manner in which the Sudan Party had conducted itself and its anti-Fulani stance, it is not surprising that Lugard and his successors were cautious in their relationships with missionaries. Circumstances forced them to rule through those very Islamic rulers whom the missionaries were condemning. Lugard desired to use as little force as possible in establishing British control. Missionaries posed a serious threat to his plans. He, however, was the son of missionaries and far from anti-missionary in his sentiments. Furthermore, he was quite aware of the contributions that voluntary agencies could make to the development of Northern Nigeria, and at a very small cost to the government. Therefore, he sought for a mission group with him he could work.

Education suffered in the Home because of the Government's concern that the Home pay its own way. Children were often apprenticed out to various Government Departments as laborers or artisans to learn a trade. Some wards were sent to other African colonies. It is true that, because of previous sad experiences, the Government took precautions for the safety and well-being of their wards, inspecting conditions or requiring other that the Governments of other British colonies do so on their behalf when children were assigned as wards to other West African British colonies. Eventually and inevitably, many of the children became wards of missionaries; some of the youngsters even went to England as wards of various people.

According to the SUM the idea of establishing a Freed Slaves' Home in connection with the Sudan United Mission was first suggested by one of the Government officials some three years ago. There is at present a home at the Government Headquarters at Zungeru, but the district in which most of the slaves are liberated is so far away, and the children who are set free are in such an emaciated condition, that about half of them die on their way to the Home, or shortly after their arrival. It is not thought advisable that the Sudan United Mission should be burdened with providing the necessary buildings and food for the liberated slaves, though the Mission will gladly undertake the support of the Teachers and Superintendents of the Home.

Here is an important difference between the SUM and the British Administration. The Administration had to work with the Fulani emirs and Sultan. The SUM, together with most missionaries, was dedicated to the conversion of Muslims and the breaking of the hegemony over the Hausa and other subject peoples. It is a significant difference, and yet, each for its own reasons, the Administration and the SUM worked together in relative harmony. For the SUM the Home provided a lasting, benevolent presence, and work the Administration deemed necessary. For the Administration the Home provided an essential service, technical training, as well as a means for keeping an eye on the missionaries and keeping them busy and away from sensitive contact with the Muslims.

Expatriate Society in Nigeria

It is important to put the situation in Northern Nigeria in the early years of the 20th Century in greater perspective; namely, that of expatriate society. There are a number of characteristics that distinguish expatriate societies from similar groups. Most obvious is the fact that expatriates come from another area, one that provides support, and one to which they ostensibly can return, sooner or later, when they finish their tour of duty. Indeed, "tour of duty" is quite an accurate description of expatriate perception of the definition of the situation. As Van Baal (1972: 87) makes clear in his own case, he went to the Netherlands East Indies because it was his moral duty to do so in order to serve mankind. Although further empirical work is necessary, it is probable that expatriates are not demographically or in value-orientation representative of their home areas. Thus, they tend to present a false and outdated version of their home societies to indigenous people. Furthermore, their contacts with those people are along pre-selected routes, congruent with their occupation of dominant power positions. Finally, although colonial officials, missionaries, indigenous staff, recognized representative of local people, servants, and the occasional anthropologist frequently differed bitterly, there were a number of instances in which overt disagreements were not tolerated, for each segment within the expatriate stratum had too much at stake in the preservation of the structure to endanger its maintenance.

The actual religious, demographic, and political situation into which the British came are important to an understanding of the patterns that they established. To put it concretely: without an understanding of the situation in which the British consolidated their rule it is impossible to understand the structure and functioning of the non-settler colonial society that Nigeria became. In 1910 there were 338 Europeans in Northern Nigeria, 120 of whom were merchants (Ajayi, Ab/p. *12/2:14).* In 1911 there were 678 Europeans in a population of 8,115,981. They constituted .00835 percent of the population, a figure that increased slightly in the census of 1921 to .01138 percent and to .01595 percent in 1931. The actual proportion of Europeans in the population in 1921 and 1931 was 1,168 of 10,259,993 and 1,825 of 11,434,924. Perhaps a more graphic illustration of the relative size of the two communities is given by a comparison of the number of Europeans and Nigerians per square mile. In 1911, there were .00265 Europeans per square mile compared with 31.74 Nigerians. In 1921 the figures were .00447 compared with 39.33. 1931's figures showed .0069958 to 40.58 (Brooke, 1933: 1). In short, the expatriate community was a face-to-face one, one that was both absolutely and relatively small.

Kirk-Green states that the rapidity of Islam's twentieth century expansion and the difference between Islam among the Kanuri, Yoruba, and Hausa. Among the Kaouri, Islam is deep and of long duration. Whereas it is a religion among the Yoruba, it is a civilization among the Hausa. The rapid spread of Islam in Hausaland, from 5 percent of the population in 1900 to 80 percent in 1950, resulted from British policy favoring Islam. After the British conquest, Islam was no longer viewed by the Hausa as the religion of the Fulani. Rather they viewed it as an alternate civilization, useful in opposition to western influence, and one honored by British policy.

One of the things to make clear is that until the British occupation Islam in West Africa was largely an aristocratic religion, professed by the ruling class who only attempted to impose it on their subjects in the early stages of the end of the 18th and beginning of the 19th centuries (Trimingham, Ab:P12/1:8:19). The distinction between sacred and secular, deeply imbedded in western culture, is antithetical to the Islamic state structure. Ironically, the Christian missionary has been one of the prime factors working toward distinguishing the two. That separation, which Trimingham (Ab:PI2/1:8:31) sums up as the "individual morality" of the missionary, was viewed by Muslims and non-Muslims in Northern Nigeria as a menace to societal stability.

The early situation, then was one in which there were very few expatriates. Originally, almost half of these were traders, who had exercised quasi-political functions before the establishment of the protectorate. The minuscule force of government officials was dependent on securing local cooperation for their efforts. Although missionaries could not cavalierly be excluded from the north, their work could be hindered, for they clearly presented a hindrance to the effective and smooth cooperation of Islamic officials. Given the face to face nature of the British community, much of the interaction takes on clear cut characteristics, typical of many of the societies which anthropologists are more accustomed to studying. In brief, conflicts clearly reveal underlying structural characteristics.

Thus, Rattray's (1934) hypothesis regarding indirect rule assumes added force when one understands that indirect rule operated in a small-scale expatriate society. Basically, Rattray (1934: 26.27) suggested

> . . . that, thirty or forty years ago, when the science of anthropology was still in its infancy, had the European conquerors of Northern Nigeria encountered such a state of society [that of West Africans] . . . they would have had neither the knowledge, nor the means, nor the time to have comprehended it, and, in consequence, Indirect Rule, as we understand it would have been almost impossible of introduction. The complexity of a so-called "primitive" tribal society would have been unintelligible to them, the intimately related social units would have seemed lacking in cohesion, nothing worthy of the name constitution or state would have been apparent. . . . It was inevitable . . . that the point of view, the only point of view, ever put forward to the British Government in those early days must have been that of this upper-ruling class—this alien aristocracy—the Fulani, this foreign minority among the millions of inarticulate subjects over whom for a

hundred years these invaders had wielded what was probably only a very nominal suzerainty.

In short, the result of Indirect Rule was the strengthening of Fulani rule in a way predictable through the application of Smith's theory of the plural society.

Indeed, Palmer's (1934: 37-48) response to Rattray is revealingly instructive. He accused Rattray of being pro-Hausa and anti-Fulani, concluding his attack by citing an un-named "learned member of the Nigerian Legislature" who complained "that he could never find out the difference between an Anthropologist and a Secretary for Native Affairs." Both, according to Palmer, were troublesome creatures who threaten a carefully balanced governing arrangement.

The point is that colonial society in Nigeria was quite complex. It was not a case of "the British" vs. "the Africans." Quite clearly neither "the British" nor "the Africans" formed a monolithic group. Rattray made explicit the alliance between colonial officials and Fulani elite. In addition, he demonstrated the simplified selective perception which enable the British to rule an area notable for its ethnographic complexity. Quite simply, British political officers accepted the Fulani's idealized version of political reality, one that those whom the Fulani conquered never accepted. Furthermore, because of its advantage in easing their rule, the British political corps solidified Fulani rule at the very time it was most in danger of collapsing.

Conversely, because of their personal contacts with indigenous peoples, missionaries, anthropologists, and secretaries for native affairs were in excellent positions to challenge this mutually convenient arrangement between Fulani and British colonial officers and its consequent distortion of reality. In turn, of course, missionaries, anthropologists, and secretaries for native affairs had perceptual biases of their own related to the interests and allegiances of their positions. Consequently, competing versions of reality entered the colonial arena. Furthermore, although colonial officials had power to limit internal opposition, those whom they opposed frequently brought countervailing power to bear in Great Britain. It is, in fact, this extension of disputes and the resulting appeal to power ultimately residing in the metropolitan center that makes the concept of the "expatriate society" a useful tool. In its light, the Lucy Memorial Freed Slaves' Home becomes more intelligible as does its importance.

The story of the Sudan Party and its relationship with Lugard makes the role of the SUM even more manifest. The pattern for colonial/missionary relations was set by G. W. Brooke's Sudan Party (1890-1892). That party was inspired by Gordon's anti-Mahdist campaign in the Sudan, and the fear that the Mahdi would rise in Nigeria. The CMS sent 11 Cambridge and Oxford graduates to Northern Nigeria, the largest single party they had ever sent to one area. The Sudan Party's attempt at cultural conversion failed miserably. Not only were their premises incorrect, but their protection against disease was tragically inadequate. They were intensely anti-Fulani and perpetuated the myth that all Hausa were nominal Muslims eagerly awaiting the liberation of Christianity, a myth that plagued missionary relationships with northern Nigerians for years.

The ultimate failure of the Sudan Party, ravished by illness and death, only spurred other missionary efforts. In 1891 a Hausa Association was formed in memory of J. A. Robinson of the Sudan Party. The real reason for its foundation was the conversion of Hausa. Goldie encouraged its foundation, for he had begun to appreciate that the government could use missionaries to build hospitals and promote education and other voluntary activities. Thus, Goldie helped establish that very pattern when he "gave" one hundred freed slaves to the missions for conversion, encouraging missionary belief that the "Sword of Steel" would go before the "Sword of Faith." The 1896 Bida War, in missionary eyes, became the precursor of what was to come.

It was the immediate cause for the 1898 expedition of the Hausaland Mission to Hausa settlements in Tripoli, for added to missionary hatred of the Fulani and Islam, was their fear and hatred of French Roman Catholics who were threatening to take over Northern Nigeria. One of the men in that party was Dr. Walter Miller, whose missionary career is itself a commentary on the development of British policy in Northern Nigeria. Although Miller's endeavors were in many ways atypical of missionary work, and he personally was at least unique, it is for these reasons that his work is so important in exposing relationships within the expatriate community that otherwise remain implicit. Miller was one of those people who had a knack for forcing those who possess "potential" power into converting it to "actual" power, consequently easing its analysis.

Quite early Miller appreciated the importance of attempting to maintain close ties with the administration, ties which he hoped would facilitate his work, or at least allow him relative freedom in ignoring directives. His peculiar relationship with Lugard deserves a complete analysis, one beyond the scope of this work. As early as 1899, Miller was lavish in his praise of the new high commissioner, a non-Christian son of missionaries. In turn, Lugard was grateful for Miller's role in gaining the allegiance of Zaria in 1902, just two years after Miller's arrival. That allegiance allowed Lugard's man to defeat Abadie Nagwananchi of Kontagora and to consolidate British control of the north. In turn, Lugard allowed Miller to establish a mission within Zaria itself.

1903 has been chosen as a period to describe relationships because it is the middle of Lugard's first rule, one in which what was to become fixed dogma was still fluid necessity. The mission community was male, as Bargery's letters to the CMS director, Baylis, make clear. Bargery was requesting permission to marry and take his wife to the mission station. He had been in the northern mission two years and four months, a period equal to that of anyone else. His arguments in favor of marriage for missionaries and the assignment of women to the field are valuable in understanding the mission society of the early days. Personally, he argued, there was a danger of not returning to the field, for his future brother-in-law opposed his missionary work; his fiancee might lose her faith if left in that situation. More generally, there was a need for female nurses and doctors. Men could not do a good deal of work in Nigeria's Islamic areas. Unless women were converted, much of the effort will be wasted. Significantly, Bargery suggested that the resident of Zaria's advice be asked.

The issue was the subject of a torrid debate and Miller sent a memo to the CMS which sheds light on day to day relations in the north. Briefly, arguments in favor of women in the missions were that there was a general peace, and the Mahdi presented no real problem. Furthermore, roads were improved, and whites were seen on every journey. As a result of the general peace and improved transportation, housing was more comfortable, for one could furnish the inside in European fashion while keeping the outside in the "native" style. Miller argued that there certainly was work for women to do. The hospital at Zungeru, for example, needed female nurses beyond the single one who worked there. Most importantly, women were needed to set an example for young children.

The fearfully wicked character of all women, even to the little girls— they are ten times more immoral that [sic] the men—makes it impossible if we want the little lads who are about us to grow up healthy and clean to let them have anything to do with these women. The need for a Christian home as an exemplar led Miller to write that he favored mothers first over wives, an obvious slap at Bargery. That there was, however, a need to prove that married men were not homosexuals, Miller admitted. Furthermore, he grudgingly conceded that some good men might refuse to come to the mission field if their wives were left behind, but that might not be a real loss.

There were some arguments against allowing any woman to come to the mission area. Mission life had a pioneer nature to it. Roads were bad from July to October. No schools were yet planned for the foreseeable future. Opposition to missionaries was still strong. Finally; the possibility of loneliness was great, for no band of lady workers was yet possible because of the necessity of offering them protection. Finally, Miller offered the following regulations pending approval by the committee of the use of female missionaries. There should be at least four women, with reinforcements available. Each woman should be free of organic diseases, "Specially those peculiar to women." None should be under the age of 27 or 28, and at least one should be a "strapping old maid," who should be the group leader. No romances should be encouraged, nor should any publicity be given. Work would consist of elementary work, specifically "in the kindergarten style," and nursing and dispensing.

Quite obviously, Miller preferred unmarried clergy, and the parallels between early CMS stations and later Roman Catholic ones are quite suggestive. His authoritarian role is clearly evident in the virtual open rebellion he caused in 1903. The immediate point at issue was the binding nature of his instructions. These essentially would have given Miller absolute control over all missionaries and their households. Bargery led a successful opposition to his absolute rule. In 1903 there was no permanent station. About 50 people attended services. All seven of the missionaries were university people. Preference for public school graduates with varsity training was a common British trait. The normal tour of duty was two and one-half years, followed by home leave. Relations with the government, which in 1903 meant Lugard, were carefully cultivated. In fact, Miller sent Lugard 19 pages of typed instructions in which he advocated changes in medical, moral and economic areas, with the use of force if needed. He complained of the hostility of government officials, and then he flatly stated that he was going to Kano and Katsina.

This missive of Miller's upset Lugard, who wrote to Baylis on 5 September to comment on Miller's long memo. In the course of that response a number of important issues were addressed. First, he was not opposed to direct rule, but with the staff and money at his disposal, there was no alternative. Although he did not trust the Fulani, necessity dictated that he work through them. To that end officials familiar with Hausa and local customs were needed. Personally, he favored Christian missions, but progress must be made in conjunction with local conditions. This was not the time to anger the Fulani. In short, stay away from Kano and Katsina (Lugard to Baylis, 5 Sept., 1903, from Surrey). On 27 October he sent Baylis another letter warning that he would not support missionaries in Kano or Katsina with force. Missionaries should stick to pagan zones, for he had given his word to keep them out of Muslim territories. In point of fact, neither statement was true. Lugard had earlier rescued Miller's ill-fated expedition to Kano and would have done so again. Furthermore, he had not promised to keep missionaries out of Islamic areas.

Whereas Miller clearly wanted to work among Hausa only, his colleagues were perfectly willing and eager to go in pairs to villages of non-Hausa. Miller himself visited eight to twelve villages of non-Hausa in two tours of seven days each. In this work, their servants aided the missionaries. Unfortunately, no one has yet analyzed the role of the young male servant in missionary work. Certainly, Miller was quite clear in his hopes that these young men, such as his Audu, would be catalysts in the coming Hausa conversion. Despite his close ties with Audu, Miller still believed in the fact of European superiority to the Hausa, a view he modified in his later life. In 1903, however, the highest praise he could give was that someone had acted "Almost like a white man" (Miller to Baylis, 11 June, 1903, CMS: G3 Ag/07/1903; Nos. 1-42, Reel Number 214).

Neither Miller nor Lugard, despite close ties, was lulled by the other's sincere friendship into misjudging his motives. Miller urged Baylis on 11 June to keep the distinction between the mission and the government clear. Any confusion in the peoples' minds between the two was detrimental. It must be stressed, however, that the relationship between missionaries and government was multiplex. Although missionaries might be a nuisance, they did perform valuable work at low cost to the government. For example, medical work figured quite prominently in the mission. Again and again, Druitt's medical skill is praised in letters. Lugard's letter to Hans Vischer, head of education for the northern provinces (MSS British Empire S76: 11 January, 1914) discussed the complexity of missionary contributions in the field of education. At the beginning

Lugard emphasized the lack of resources at the government's disposal. Missionaries were all too eager to fill the gap. The Ugandan experience, however, marred by Christian rivalry was held to be instructive. Therefore, a number of variables must be checked: the form of the missionary, the teacher, and the consent of the parents. Furthermore, spheres of influence should be established. A hint of a *quid pro quo* is found in Lugard's irritation that Islam was allowed into pagan areas where Christianity was excluded. More ironic is the fact that Palmer had invoked Lugard's Indirect Rule to keep missionaries out of areas where Lugard would have welcomed them. In offering a rare glimpse of his inner thoughts, he wrote: purely secular Education divorced from Moral Instruction and from Religion. Among races who have not the tradition and the ethical standards which centuries of Christian teaching and environment have produced in Europe, infallibly produces a class of young men and women who lack reverence alike for their parents, their social superiors, their employers, or the Government. They lack self restraint and control, and they lack the foundation on which all the highest and best work in the world is based whether of public and civic usefulness, or of private incentive and effort.

Consequently, Lugard ordered moral education in the secondary schools. He further ordered contact with the Moral Education League in England and the securing of their publications. In addition, he asked that hours for optional religious education be certified, and that the spheres of influence for various religious missions be established (MSS Brit. Em s76). The impetus given by Lugard's actions is clearly seen. In 1913 there were 38 mission stations in the northern provinces. In 1917 there were more than 60, including churches in Kaduna, Zaria, and Jos (Secretary, N. P., to Private Secretary to H. E., Governor-General, 17 January 1918, MSS Brit. Em s76). Lugard, however, did not remain in power long and those who replaced him continued the canonization of Indirect Rule. Their motives may well have been mixed, but as Ayandele (1967: 145-52) rightly argues, missionaries presented political problems and were quick to cause difficulties wherever they went. Miller's expedition to Kano in 1901 was a colossal blunder. Merchants were opposed to missionaries, moreover, because they denounced the liquor trade and the general comportment of merchants. Ayandele (ibid.) makes clear that the policy of men like Girouard and Temple, however, was anti-missionary because, however much they admired Islamic culture, they were afraid of missionary exposure of their shortcomings.

Indirect Rulers had much to hide from the gaze of the British public, through probable revelations by the missionaries to the British press. Many of the Residents were overbearing in their attitudes to the natives and condoned many acts of oppression by the chiefs and emirs. The officials were, in a missionary observer's view, "brave English officers, genial, good natured, but utterly ungodly, all living loose lives, all having women brought to them wherever they are." Missionaries also felt that in the pacification of the territory much bloodshed that could have been avoided, the report of which never reached the Colonial Office, occurred. In places where missionaries were allowed to establish themselves many people who could not obtain redress for wrongs from Residents flocked to missionaries for "advice" (ibid.: 151).

The missionary mentioned in the quotation was, of course, Miller and the implacable opposition he had to the slaughter of Nigerians, exemplified in the Hadeja campaign, earned him the hatred of numerous administrators. In short, under Percy Girouard what had been necessity for Lugard became policy. The response that J. F. Matthews (MSS Afr s783, 27 July, 1924) gave to his brother, Basil Matthews's book *The Clash of Colour* (1926: London, Cargate Press) serves as a clear example of the attitude of colonial officers to outside criticism,

> The difficulty with you righteously indignant once is to put yourselves in our place, to visualize the enormous areas and distances involved, the fewness of communication facilities such as railroads, roads and telegraph wires and (most of all) the attitude and mentality of the inhabitants and the consequent difficulty of effect of one's action on the minds of Englishmen.

Matthews went on to bemoan the result of "half-baked education" on the wrong natives who then exploited their illiterate brothers. That hostile attitude toward those who let the side down was applied against missionaries, anthropologists, and others who publicly deviated from the office line. Although the American anthropologist Oberg worked in East Africa, his (Oberg, 1972: 77-78) comments apply to Northern Nigeria.

> Nothing in my past had prepared me to live within barriers as rigid as those which separated Europeans and natives or to come to terms with the harsh punishment sometimes meted out to natives. . . . In retrospect it is easy to see how such conditions enforce conformity and limit the freedom of the anthropologist. . . . It was in Africa that I first

encountered culture shock as a personal problem and, I might add, one which also troubled some of the British colonial officials. However, I had the problem of adjusting to two subcultures: that of British colonial officialdom and that of the native people of Ankole. . . . At the time the government station at Mbarara in the district of Ankole consisted of eight British officials. Life in the station was governed by strict routine. Office hours were from eight to one, then lunch and a siesta until four in the afternoon. I was soon informed that house visits during siesta hours were strictly tabu. At four most of the men and women went to the nine-hole golf-course. . . . My relations with the British officials were strained until I adapted myself to their three primary social interests, which were golf, hunting, and the sundowner circuit. . . . At a sundowner, the quiet officiousness of the British was replaced by talkative friendliness.

Summary

Expatriate society in Northern Nigeria is significant for many reasons. Chief among these is the fact that Northern Nigeria provided the prototype for indirect rule, a situation that originally developed from necessity as an *ad hoc* set of social relationships and then became transformed into a quasi-sacred cultural set of principles. These principles determined when, where, how, and with whom interactions could take place. Furthermore, Northern Nigeria had the reputation for being the locus of the best overseas administrators, and, therefore, of being another type of model. Finally, Northern Nigeria was not a settler colony. The number of expatriates was always small and the categories to which each expatriate belonged clearly delineated.

The British established colonial government in a sparsely settled area containing numerous minority ethnic groups. To govern this area they had few officers, fewer of whom were well-trained. They quickly formed an alliance with the ruling Fulani, whose views regarding political, social, and economic reality it was convenient to accept. Within the British ruling group there were people who threatened the fundamental perception of reality that justified Indirect Rule. While each group that differed from the dominant section of the British segment did so for different and at times antagonistic reasons, each shared the fact of support from the metropolitan area and could not simply be crushed or ignored.

Each category had its own reasons for being in Nigeria but all were subordinate to the cause of empire, for quite clearly no expatriate could be in Nigeria without the permission of the government. Therefore, while there were conflicts within the expatriate community, there were no disagreements regarding British right to rule. For example, while Miller quite openly argued that the cross should follow the sword, he never objected to the right of the sword to be where it was. Although the specifics of the operation of government might be questioned, the right to govern never was.

These arguments, however, were not quibbles. They were real conflicts, ones which determined patterns of interaction. Missionaries tended to view the Fulani as "the enemy," frequently failing to distinguish between ruling and cattle Fulani, while tending to idealize the Hausa. The British officers did the opposite. The examples given in the body illustrate both "type" errors. The Hausa-Fulani alliances or the intricacies of the *jihad* tended to be victims of ideological bias. Quite expectedly, the ruling elite of the British and local authorities increasingly identified their causes, and missionaries tended to identify with non-Fulani and non-Muslims.

Within the expatriate community arguments, regarding means could be carried outside Northern Nigeria. Examples are given that clearly show that appeals to the governor could succeed. At the same time, one could always appeal to London. The final success of the Church of the Brethren provides a dear example of the impact metropolitan politics could have on policy in the north. Furthermore, there were conflicts within each segment of expatriate society. The administrative services were no more monolithic than were the missionaries. Again, while each presented a unified front toward other segments, and all did so toward Nigerians, each was internally differentiated. To those familiar with the work of Evans-Pritchard (1940), Gluckman (1954), or Durkheim and Mauss (1963), this fact will not appear strange. To many analysts, however, plural societies have been treated as rather static entities whose members from constituent parts met in stereotypical encounters.

What is being suggested is that a more dynamic perspective will prove useful. Specifically, conflict within each segment demands analysis and is as problematic as agreement. Over what issues will there be splits within each constituent of each of the plural segments? Over which issue will there be agreements? The use of the, Mahdi as a bogey-man illustrates the use of appeal to a common enemy to compel unity in the face of opposition. At root plural societies last because members of the ruling segment agree to confine their disagreements within the plural framework.

They also last because alliances are formed across segments. The administration formed alliances with the old ruling elite, thereby changing a system under the guise of preserving it. These alliances and those of the missionaries with enemies of the system were the results of differential perceptions of reality, within and between each segment. A host of problems in this area have only begun to be explored.

In addition, the entire issue of ties to the metropolitan areas and the outside world demand as much attention as those of differential perceptions and patterns of interaction. Van den Bergh's (1973) insight, based on his research at the University of Ibadan, that conflict within an elite segment is confined within reasonable limits and works to preserve the system because of basic agreement on ultimate organizational goals, including its preservation, holds true for the colonial situation. Examination of the Lucy Memorial Freed Slaves' Home allows further elaboration of this thesis in largely unexplored case.

Chapter Seven

Promoting the Lucy Memorial Freed Slaves' Home

The SUM had a number of ways for promoting the Home. One of the more effective means of promotion was its use of its organ *The Lightbearer*. This magazine gave a good deal of its space to the Lucy Memorial Freed Slaves' Home. It made sure that children received the news of the Home as well as adults. Children were filled in on the progress of missionaries. The addition of five new missionaries was a matter for rejoicing as they were sent "to reinforce, at the front, those who have been giving good service to the Master's cause." These new recruits included three people from South Africa, two women and a man, as well as "Mr. Ghev and myself, who are on our way out from England on board the S.S. Dakar." Note the warlike language. They are recruits going to the front. The battle is with the Muslims who have enslaved non-Muslims, including innocent children.

These missionaries plan to meet at the coast and go up to Rumasha, the site of the Freed Slaves' Home. The three women will stay at the Home to work. The men will go elsewhere. The children are given a detailed and colorful account of the voyage to Nigeria. No detail is too small to recount.

Now, you will wonder what I noticed first of all about our new home. It was a little flag with a blue margin and a white inside, which was flying at the foremast head. This little flag is what the sailors call the "Blue Peter," and when it is flown at the masthead means that the ship "is about to proceed to sea." And so, as she was flying this flag when

she came alongside the landing-stage, everyone knew that they had no
time to lose, but must get their baggage quickly on board, and make all
their final preparations for our long voyage. As soon, then, as the ship
was fast at the quay, and the three gangways in their places, porters,
with luggage on their shoulders, postmen, with mail-bags, and passen-
gers, with the friends who had come to see them off, were soon scur-
rying up on to the deck, and for about an hour the "Dakar" was transformed into what much resembled a beehive full of busy bees. Several
friends came to see us off, and we tried to make them as comfortable
as we could in our little cabin, and shortly before 11 o clock two of
them.

Of course, the missionaries began their journey with a prayer for the
safety of the ship and the success of their work. Thus, the following
excerpt was typical of the magazine's approach. It is from a regular
column for the "matron" of the Home. She begins her column by addressing her "nieces and nephews" and asking about their happy holidays. Quickly, she mentions how terrible the situation is for African
children, evoking sympathy in order to gain their support for aid to these
children as part of their evangelical duty.

The time which you will have spent, I am sure happily, during your
holidays would enable you to appreciate more the sorrows and tempta-
tions of the little black boys and girls in Africa, who have no kind
friends, and some of them no homes of their own. You will want to do
all you can to make them happy, through the knowledge of Jesus and
His gospel. You will be delighted, as we were, to hear that, at last the
little Freed Slave Children have reached the new home at Rumasha,
and that they are now under the tender care of the missionaries there.
There are about 115 girls and 47 boys, and they form quite a big
family. I am sure that you will remember them in your daily prayer
that they may grow up Christian boys and girls. Mrs. Paterson gives a
very interesting account of their arrival. You will also see a very interesting letter from Mr. Kemp-Welch in this number. He is, probably,
now in the Freed Slaves' Home, and has promised to write us some
stories about them, and send some photos as soon as he can get them.
I have received 10/- more for our own little Freed Slave from a kind
friend in Perthshire.

There were stories for children by Mr. Patterson. These stories were
very descriptive, colorful and filled with details of daily life in Nigeria.
There were generally children somewhere in the tale and references to

how similar the Northern Nigerian landscape was to the Holy Land. The following story is a typical example.

> One day when Mr. Martin wanted to go to a big market, in the country, beyond Rumasha town, I accompanied him. We went first to Rumasha and passed right through it. (By) the North gate we found a poor leprous man begging. He looked so sad and was in a very bad condition. All we could do was to give him some money. It would be fine if the Church could be trusted again with the gift of healing, but it seems she cannot stand that yet.

> Leaving Rumasha we found the broadest road I have yet seen leading out into a fine open country, gradually rising. We could see for many miles an interminable bush, and far back to the North some good hills. We thought we were going to be late for the market, as we met many women and children returning with huge loads on their heads, but when we got in sight of Gwari hill we also heard that the market was in full swing, not because anyone told us, but across the intervening valley a sound, like a small tornado, rolled up to greet us. It was the sound of many voices. So down we went into the valley and up the mound on the other side, and what a sight met our eyes.

> On a circular space on the top of a hill, with a goodly number of trees which afforded shade, we found some hundreds of people. Most of the traders were women, some of them very old and ugly, while others were young, and a few really handsome. All wore arranged in great circles, with the various goods laid out on the ground. These goods consisted of all sorts of food stuffs and wearing apparel. Some of the food did not look very nice, and when we came to a native restaurant we did not sit down to regale ourselves, I thought the lady in charge seemed anxious to deal. The Gwari women seem quite a different type from any we have seen before, being large and clumsy, and having their heads shaved. The whole market seemed to be under the supervision of the King of Rumasha, as one of his officers, an immense man, was going about with a hippo hide whip dangling from his arm, which in his wand of office as chief of market. He most carefully followed us round and saw we were well treated. He is the big man, with the large turban, who acted as king's herald when the King called on us. Since our visit, some women . . . have been coming here regularly with sacks of beans which Mr. Martin is buying for provision for the children when they come. The (mix) of the many voices was extraordinary. I suppose I can safely say even I could recognize (many different languages).

Missionaries are presented as living very exotic lives among uncommon but somehow familiar people. Mundane activities occur in strange settings. There were attempts made to involve children in raising funds for the little children at the Freed Slaves' Home. Little boxes were placed in the children's section of the *Lightbearer*. The jots below represented 24 shillings. 80 shillings were needed to support a second "Little Freed Slave."

O	O	O	O	O	O	O	O O
O	O	O	O	O	O	O	O

There is a fine description about the arrival of "the black boys and girls to the Home." Patterson discusses what the children eat, how they play, and what they do in the Home. He begins with a discussion of the arrival of the first children to enter the Home. "They arrived in one of the Government steamers on Monday, 9th August. It was very wet that day, and, as our landing stage was not big enough, they had to cross to the shore on a large plank, and then splash through the mud as best they could."

In the conversational style of the piece, the narrator points out that the children did not mind going through the mud because they "do not wear either shoes or stockings!" African matrons and an African male assistant who brought animals with them accompanied the children. Paterson reports that "when the rain stopped and I went down to the beach I met troops of children, some leading a most refractory goat or kid, others with fowls, turkeys, geese, or pigeons."

The courtesy of the children was impressive and moved the missionary. The girls curtseyed and wished her "Good morning, Ma." The boys saluted. Then follows a brief sermon to the readers. "It was because I realized just then, from what depths of degradation and misery and pain those young lives had been saved, and what possibilities lie in our hands in the way of making or marring their future usefulness to God and their country. You must all pray, dear children, that our missionaries may be given all the wisdom and grace and patience that is needed to train so many children."

The SUM saw these children as the future of Nigeria and their own future. These children will be trained to be servants of the Lord. "We must train them, not only to be truthful and clean and honest, but to love our dear Lord and serve Him who has saved them from slavery, and sent them to the "Lucy Memorial" Home where they can be happy and well cared for." The training was rather rigorous but not cruel and a vast improvement of slave conditions.

The day began at 5:00 a.m. Children then had breakfast at 6:00 a.m. Then the workday began in earnest. Older girls did what was then considered women's work: laundry, shaking out bed mats and blankets, getting the lunch ready, and whatever else needed doing. The whatever else included the following. "Others lead the goats out to pasture, or feed the other animals, and still others take charge of five or six smaller girls who keep clearing the compound of weeds or large stones, or carry gravel to keep the path to the kitchen nice and dry, or go down to the Benue for water for their daily bath, or for use in the kitchen." In turn, older boys worked with the male assistant. Their job was to clear roads and farms.

However, there was time for children to play. Soccer was the favorite of the boys. In fact, a pitch is made for donations to the Home of old soccer balls. There was also time to pray. "After their evening meal they sing hymns with Mr. Maxwell as long as he will sing with them, and then they have evening prayers, spread their blankets on the floor, cover themselves with another blanket and go off to sleep. They all seem very happy to be with us." It seems that they all looked forward to Saturday when they participated in drilling exercises.

There were many other stories that drew children into the romance of the mission station and the plight of the Freed Slave children. Patterson had a knack for providing details in her narrative that captured the feel of being in the Nigerian missions.

From Lokoja (look in your map of Africa and see where it is) we had to travel for three days and two nights in a barge that had an awning over part of it and curtains that could be drawn down when a storm was coining, or when you wanted to be screened from the blazing sun. How would you like to sleep all night in such a boat, or on a sand bank as many of our Missionaries have to do when the boat is too small for them to sleep in? Shortly after we arrived here the Hausa king came to see us and brought us a present. We showed him the little organ we brought out here to play hymns for the freed slaves when they come, and he was greatly pleased. Our old friend Tom interpreted for us. He had never seen a white lady before. I talked quite a long time with him and told him why we had left our children and home to come to help to teach them about Jesus, who loves them so dearly.

The missionaries showed the emir pictures of their children, which he seemed to like. The emir returned their visit soon after. A bit of English pride crept into Patterson's tale.

He rode on his horse (not a very handsome animal as compared with our English horses). It had a most elaborate head dress of red and black cloth and bits of tin. The king's man had on a wonderful turban and a large straw hat on top of that. The king himself had on a beautiful green, gold-embroidered robe.

The usual pleasantries took place, coffee, bread, biscuits—and preaching about Jesus and his love. One wonders what a devout Muslim emir made of the situation. He appears to have taken it in stride and with that great courtesy typical of Hausa-Fulani rulers. Probably, there was a bit of amusement toward the missionaries.

There is a quick recounting of a young teen who escaped from slavery. The boy had been sold in Rumasha. His master had kept him in a locked room from which the boy escaped. He found his way to the Home where the missionaries told him he was now free. The little vignette closes with a call for the young readers to pray for him and to help him preach to others about his good fortune. The boy is the oft-cited Tom. There is a conscious effort to involve youngsters in the mission, to convey the adventure of spreading the Good News, and to inculcate the necessity for doing so. Thus, the Freed Slaves' Home is made real through interesting vignettes.

Chapter Eight

Conclusion

Understanding the dynamics and structure of the Lucy Memorial Freed Slaves' Home is important in itself. It is also important for the illumination it sheds on the understanding of expatriate society. The Home could only have existed within the colonial system known as indirect rule, where the fiction prevailed of a Dual Mandate between the British and their subject or native rulers. Those who ran the Home walked a thin line, often following policies of which they disapproved in order to promote policies for the good of the people whom they served. Thus, while being strongly anti-Muslim and pro-Christian, they refrained from preaching to Muslims in order to work with freed slaves and to carry out missionary work among "animists." They sought to cover over, at least publicly, differences with colonial policy and its implementation so that their work would go forward. Study of the manner in which they did so gives us an important instance of Indirect Rule in action.

In Nigeria, Ghana, and other British colonies under Indirect Rule expatriates overrepresented the upper middle class in Britain. In social class origins and value, they presented a false and outdated side of British culture. Unsurprisingly, they structured their contacts with indigenous peoples along carefully pre-selected routes. They valued, for example, proper aristocratic behavior, favoring those groups, such as the Fulani, whom they considered more refined in demeanor and nobler in tradition. Moreover, it is crucial to understand that the sacred tenets of indirect rule required local financial support for all local governmental functions, including education, in Nigeria at least, the British found it useful to posit an innate hostility between Islam and Christianity, between Western and Islamic education and practices and significantly between democracy and adherence to tradition. Furthermore, the value of studying expatriate societies transcends its significant relationship to problems of the validity and reliability of social science research because expatriate societies are only one transform of plural societies, one of many possible concrete manifestations of deeper underlying structural principles. Before social science can succeed in uncovering these structural principles, further empirical research and clearer conceptualization of the problem are needed. Beidelman (1974: 235-36) states the situation succinctly:

> Anthropologists tend to neglect those groups nearest themselves, and in the scurry to conduct relevant research, a broad area of great theoretical interest has been passed by. Almost no attention was ever paid by anthropologists to the study of colonial groups such as administration, missionaries, or traders. Anthropologists may have spoken about studying total societies, but they did not seem to consider their compatriots as subjects for wonder and analysis . . . colonial structures may be viewed as variants of a tar broader type, that of the complex bureaucratic organization.

Beidelman's perceptive categorization of expatriate colonial society as a subtype or variant of Weber's "complex bureaucratic organization" parallels M. G. Smith's (1969: 434) contention that colonial society is but one important variant of the plural society. Smith's (ibid. 444-45) further discussion regarding the types of pluralism suggests a useful research approach:

Structural pluralism consists in the differential incorporation of connectivities segregated as social sections and characterized by institutional divergences. Cultural pluralism consists in variable institutional diversity without corresponding collective segregation. Social pluralism involves the organization of institutionally dissimilar collectivities and corporate sections or segments whose boundaries demarcate distinct communities and systems of social action. The differential incorporation that institutes structural pluralism is found only in societies where institutionally diverse collectivities are set apart as corporate social sections of unequal status and resources. In these conditions, if the ruling sections form a numerical minority of the aggregate, we find the plural society in the classic form described by Furnival.

Additionally, social scientists have described Furnival's classic plural society, colonial society, in works of greater or lesser detail. They have failed to provide adequate descriptions, however, of the workings of colonial society in non-settler communities. Furthermore, these descriptions, with rare exceptions, tend to be outsiders' views which typically describe either the subordinate sections of the plural society or contact areas. Rarely does any social scientist analyze the dominant stratum. Indeed, it is rather suggestive that, overall, novelists such as Paul Theroux, Joyce Carey, and George Orwell have offered the best descriptions of expatriate societies, ones that compel emotional assent.

Beidelman's (1974: 235-36) recommendation that scholars focus attention on dominant segments of colonial society, using a Weberian analytic framework, can be profitably combined with a judicious use of Smith's model of structural pluralism. Significantly, these Weberian approaches not only do not logically exclude the notion of process, they profit by it. They do so because the corporate segments of the plural society are always in real or potential conflict, and, at best, any equilibrium is tenuous (Kuper, 1969: 462, 465, especially 470,475). In addition, there is a dynamic conflict within each section, one that has been, unfortunately, virtually ignored within the literature.

There is need, then, to focus on one transform of the plural society, the non-settler colonial society. There is even greater need to focus on the dominant segment of the society, the expatriate component. That segment is itself one variety of Weber's bureaucratic type. Any solution to the problem of kinds of plural societies and their underlying processes can only result from the application of theoretically derived concepts to empirical situations carefully chosen to permit the observation of the interaction of relevant variables.

Similarly, European missionaries had advocated a direct governmental role in protecting their interests. They had been upset with Goldie's separation of religion from politics and trade. There was little patience in the missionary community for his conciliatory gestures toward Muslim rulers. In fact, European missionaries attributed much of his anti-missionary attitude to his being a Jew..

In addition, the entire issue of ties to the metropolitan areas and the outside world demands as much attention as those of differential perceptions and patterns of interaction. This book has not explored that issue. Certainly, however, it has suggested that these ties were of vital importance to events within Nigeria. Appeals to those outside the north were frequent. Now it is vital to work out a typology of appeals, frequency, and success of each.

In an article that aids in that task, Lubeck (1981, 70) reminds us that:

> Colonial rule did not interfere with Islamic practices in the Sokoto Caliphate. In fact, indirect rule created an alliance between a faction of the Muslim aristocracy and the colonial state in which foreign trading firms, acting through layers of agents, linked the pre-existing peasant household and market sectors to the capitalist world economy.

The case of the Lucy Memorial Freed Slaves' Home illuminates these points clearly. The Freed Slaves' Home, run by a voluntary society, kept the government free of day-to-day involvement. The society, a union of evangelical missionaries, the Sudan United Mission, proved amenable to the restrictions the colonial government imposed on it. Although strongly anti-Muslim, the SUM contented itself with caring for those in the Home and working among "pagans" to stop the spread of Islam. Its members did not preach to Muslims but did pressure the government to abolish slavery and free those who were kept as slaves in Nigeria.

The study of the SUM's role in establishing the Home, furthermore, offers insight into the manner in which expatriates groups adapted to the exigencies of the colonial condition in order to advance their own ends. Accommodations, compromises, had to be made to fit into the total community. The question of when accommodations became betrayal of principles was a significant one and much-debated. The process which the SUM had to use sheds light on the general anti-slavery movement in Britain at the beginning of the 20th Century and the role of the evangelical movement in social reform.

Lucy herself is an individual whose work is iconic in nature. Her undercover work exposing abuses in female labor, her role in the founding of the Sudan United Mission, and her tireless efforts, leading to her premature death, for the establishment of a Freed Slaves' Home inspired much of the work of the SUM and other mission groups. Certainly, her story combines the role of the individual and that of the times in an enlightening manner. She navigated the many streams of British history, and in so doing enables us to put them into clearer perspective.

The Lucy Memorial Freed Slaves' Home, thus, was part of an overall mission plan to evangelize the non-Muslim tribes of Northern Nigeria. At each SUM station there were graduates of the Home who aided in its evangelization work, including education and medical efforts. According to Crane the SUM dispensed 50,000 medical treatments and had 60,000 school attendances yearly.

From its inception the SUM planned to make the Freed Slaves' Home a recruitment and training center for evangelists. Gibson (n.d.), for example, admitted that time was making the need for a Freed Slaves' Home less urgent. He accepted Lugard's rhetoric about slavery's abolition in Northern Nigeria. However, he quickly asserted that even though the day would come when there would be no more freed slaves to care for, the Home could be used for educational or industrial purposes. Meanwhile, there were a large number of freed slaves who urgently needed help.

Thus, the very existence of the Home was part of the accepted give and take of colonial reality in which compromises had to be made. Each participant in the negotiations of daily life gave up some ground in hopes of gaining a larger advantage down the road. In that manner, a working misunderstanding evolved in which many things were ignored so that the daily tasks could be attempted. In this somewhat messy structure order somehow emerged. It is in understanding how that order could emerge that this study makes a significant contribution.

References

Archival Material

Aberdeen: Department of Religious Studies, King's College, University of Aberdeen.

AB/P12/1:14 Ajayi, William (n. d.) *Aspects of Protestant Mission World Northern Nigeria.*

AB(f12j2:2 Crampton, E. P. T. (1967) *Christianity in the North of Nigeria.* Dublin: University of Dublin, B.D. Thesis.

Owoh, Aaron Chikwendis (1971) *C.M.S. Missions, Muslim Societies and European Trade in Northern Nigeria: 1857-1900.* Aberdeen: University of Aberdeen, Faculty of Divinity, M.A. Thesis.

AB/PI2/1:8 Trimingham, J. Spencer (1955) *Islam in West Africa.* IL Church Missionary Society

CMS: G5 Ag/07/1901l: Numbers 1-42. Red Number 214—The Hausaland Mission.

Rhodes House

MSS African S 783

MSS British Empire S76

C. O. 446/10 No. 23453. Lugard, Jebba, 16/6/1900.

Colonial Report No. 476 for 1904.

Northern Nigerian Colonial Report Number 346. 1900-1901.

Parliament Papers 1907. LIV Report on Northern Nigeria for 1905-1906. (cds. 3285 - 3).

Report on a Committee appointed by the Order of His excellency Sir Percy Girouard, High Commissioner, Northern Nigeria, to investigate matters connected with the Freed Slaves Home in Secretariat Minute Paper No. 5091/1907

Missionary Records

Gibson, Monro (n. d.) The Urgency of the Call from the Sudan. London: Marshall Brothers.

S. A. Branch of the Sudan United Mission (1908) First Annual Report. Cape Town: The Standard Press.

S. A. Branch of the Sudan United Mission (1909) Second Annual Report. Cape Town: The Standard Press.

S. A. Branch of the Sudan United Mission (1910) Third Annual Report. Cape Town: The Standard Press.

S. A. Branch of the Sudan United Mission (1911) Fourth Annual Report. Cape Town: The Standard Press.

Sudan United Mission (1908) The Lucy Memorial Freed Slaves' Home. London: Marshall Brothers.

Sudan United Mission, American Branch (1918) Report and Review, April 1921. Summit, N. J: Office of the Mission.

Sudan United Mission, American Branch (1921) Report and Review, April 1921. Summit, N. J: Office of the Mission.

Sudan United Mission, American Branch (1922) Report and Review, April 1922. Summit, N. J: Office of the Mission.

Sudan United Mission, American Branch (1923) Report and Review. Summit, N. J: Office of the Mission.

Sudan United Mission, American Branch (1924) Report and Review. Summit, N. J: Office of the Mission.

Published Material

Ajayi, J. F. A. *Christian Missions in Nigeria (1841-1891)*. Evanston: Northwestern University Press.

Asad, Talal (ed.). *Anthropology and the Colonial Encounter*. London: Ithaca Press.

Ayandele, E. A. (1970) *The Missionary Impact on Modem Nigeria*. New York: Humanities Press.

Baranowski, Shelley and Furlough, Ellen *Culture, and Identity in Modern Europe and North America*. The University of Michigan Press.

Barkow, Jerome (1970) "Processes of Group Differentiation in a Rural Area of North Central State, Nigeria." Chicago: Ph.D. Dissertation, Department of Anthropology, University of Chicago.

Barnes, Virginia Lee. *Amandine*. York: Pantheon Books, 1994.

Beidelman, T. O. (1974) "Social Theory and the Study of Christian Missions in Africa." *Africa* 44, 8: 285-49.

Boer, Jan Harm. (1979) Missionary Messengers of Liberation in a Colonial Context: A Case Study of the Sudan United Mission. Amsterdam: Rodopi.

Brooke, N. J. (1985) *Census of Nigeria,* 1931 *(Census of the Northern Provinces).* London: The Crown Agents for the Colonies.

Cohen Abner, 1985. *The Symbolic Construction of Community*, London / New York: Tavistock Publications.

——. 1976 *Two-Dimensional Man: An Essay on the Anthropology of Power and Symbolism in Complex Society.* Berkeley: University of California Press.

——. 1974 "Introduction" to *Urban Ethnicity*, ed. A. Cohen. London: Tavistock.

——. 1981. *The Politics of Elite Culture: Explorations in the Dramaturgy of Power in a Modern African Society.* Berkeley: University of California Press.

——. 1993. *Masquerade Politics: Explorations in the Structure of Urban Cultural Movements.* Berkeley: University of California Press.

Cohen Abner. 1979. "Political symbolism." *Annual Review of Anthropology* 8: 87-113.

——. 1981. *The Politics of Elite Culture: Explorations in the Dramaturgy of Power in a Modern African Society.* Berkeley: University of California Press.

Cohen, Ronald, and John Middleton, eds. 1967. *Comparative Political Systems: Studies in the Politics of Pre-Industrial Societies.* Austin: University of Texas Press. Annual Spring Meeting of the American Ethnological Society, ed. J. Helm. Seattle: University of Washington Press.

Coles, Catherine, and Mack, Beverly. 1991a. "Women in twentieth century Hausa society," in *Hausa Women in the Twentieth Century*, pp. 3-26. Madison, Wis.: University of Wisconsin Press.

Coles, Catherine, and Mack, Beverly (eds.). 1991b. Hausa Women in the Twentieth Century. Madison, Wis.: University of Wisconsin Press.

Collier, J., and S. I. Yanagisako (eds.). (1987) *Gender and Kinship; Essays toward a Unified Analysis.* Stanford: Stanford University Press.

Comaroff, John L. (1987) "Sui Genderis: Feminism, Kinship Theory, and Structural Domains." In J. F. Collier & S. J. Yanagisako [eds], *Gender and Kinship*. Stanford: Stanford University Press.

Condominus, Georges. (1978) *Ethnics and Comfort: An Ethnographer's View of His Profession*. Washington: American Anthropological Association: 1-17.

Crane, Denis. (n. d.) *A Challenge! Shall We Surrender the Sudan?* London: Sudan United Missions.

Creevey, Lucy, and Barbara Callaway. *The Heritage of Islam: Women, Religion, and Politics in West Africa*. Boulder, CO: Lynne Rienner, 1994.

Durkheim, Emile and Marcel Mauss. (1965) *Primitive Classification*, Trans. with an Introduction by Rodney Needham. Chicago: University of Chicago Press.

Echard, Nicole. (1991) "Gender relationships and religion: women in the Hausa Bori of Ader, Niger," in Catherine Coles and Beverly Mack (eds), *Hausa Women in the Twentieth Century*, pp. 207w20. Madison, Wis.: University of Wisconsin Press.

Esposito, John L. (1982) *Women in Muslim Family Law*. 1st ed. Syracuse, NY: Syracuse University Press.

Evans-Pritchard, E. E. (1940) *The Nuer*. New York: Oxford University Press.

Farber, Bernard. (1983) *Comparative Kinship Systems: A Method of Analysis*. New York: Wiley.

Farber, Bernard. (1981) *Conceptions of Kinship*. New York: Elsevier.

Fishburne, Collier and Sylvia Junko Yanagisako (eds.). *Gender and Kinship: Essays Toward a Unified Analysis*. Stanford: Stanford University Press, pp. 53-85.

Gallaway, A. D. (1960) "Missionary Impact on Nigeria." *Nigeria,* 59-65.

Gluckman, Max. (1954) *Rituals of Rebelllion in South-East Africa*. Manchester: University of Manchester Press.

Goffman, Erving. 1967 *Interaction Ritual*. Pantheon: New York.

Goffman, Erving. *The Presentation of Self in Everyday Life*. Doubleday: Garden City, New York, 1959. Goffman, Erving. 1963 *Stigma*. Prentice-Hall: Englewood Cliffs, New Jersey.

Graham, Sonia F. (1955) A History of Education in Relation to the Development of the Protectorate of Northern Nigeria, 1900-1919 with Special Reference to the Work of Hans Vischer, University of London Ph.D. thesis.

Guinness, Fanny E. (1880) "Some Are Fallen Asleep" or, the Story of Our Sixth Year at the East London Institute for Home and Foreign Mission. London: Hoddes and Staughton.

———. (1886) *The Wide World and Our Work in It*. London: Hodder and Staughton.

———. (n. d.) *Whose Fault Is It?* London: Marshall Brothers.

Guinness, H. Grattan. (1907) *Lucy Guinness Kumm, Her Life Story*. Private Printing.

Guinness, Lucy E. (n. d.) *To Help To Heal*. London: E. Marlborough & Co.

———. (1886) *Only a Factory Girl*.

———. (1889) *In the Far East, Letters from Geraldine Guinness*. London: Gilbert & Rivington.

Hekmat, Anwar. (1997) *Women and the Koran: The Status of Women in Islam*. Amherst, NY: Prometheus Books.

Heussler, Robert. (1968) *The British in Northern Nigeria*. London: Oxford University Press.

July, Robert W. (1992) *A History of the African People*. Prospect Heights, IL: Waveland.

Jones, G. L. "Social Anthropology in Nigeria during the Colonial Period." *Africaf:* 4: 280-89.

Kirk-Greene, A. H. M. (1958) "Saga of Liberty Village." *West African Review*. October: 867-869.

Kumm, Karl. (1907) *The Sudan*. London: Marshall Brothers.

———. (1910) *From Hausaland to Egypt*. London: Constable & Co.

Kumm, Lucy Guinness. (n. d.) *Oh, Love That Will Not Let Me Go: A New Year's Dream*. London: Marshall Brothers.

Kuper, Leo. (1969) "Ethnic and Racial Pluralism: Some Aspects of Polarization and Depluralization," pp. 459-487 in Leo Kuper and M. G. Smith (eds.) *Pluralism in Africa*. Berkeley: University of California Press.

Lewis, Diane. (1975) "Anthropology and Colonialism." *Current Anthropology* 14: 581-602.

London Times (1904) Dealing with Slave Raiders.

London Times (1909) Announces Opening of Freed Slaves Home (Rumasha).

Lovejoy, Paul E. (1983) *African Transformations in Slavery*. Cambridge: Cambridge University Press.

———— and Jan S. Hogendorn. (1993) *Slow Death for Slavery: The Course of Abolition in Northern Nigeria, 1897-1936*. Cambridge: Cambridge University Press.

Lugard, Frederick Lord. (1965) *The Dual Mandate in British Tropical Africa*. London: F. Cass, original 1922.

————. (1933) "Slavery in all Its Forms." *Africa* 6: 3-14.

Matthews, Basil. (1926) *The Clash of Colour*. London: Cargate Press.

Maxwell, J. L. (n. d.) *Half a Century of Grace, A Jubilee History of the SUM Sidcup*, England: SUM.

Oberg, Kavero. (1972) *Journal of the Royal African Society*. 55:57-48.

Olusanya, G. O. (1966) "The Freed Slaves' Homes—An Unknown Aspect of Northern Nigerian Social History." *Journal of the Historical Society of Nigeria* 3: 523-538.

Palmer, Sir Richmond. (1954) "Some Observations on Captain R. S. Rattray's Paper 'Present Tendencies of African Colonial Development.'"

Perham, Margery. (1960) *Lugard: The Years of Authority 1898-1945*. London: Collins Press.

Pitt, David C. (1976) "Development from Below," pp; 7-19 in David C. Pitt (ed.) *Development from Below: Anthropologists and Development Situations*. The Hague: Mouton.

Rattray, R. S. (1954) "Present Tendencies of African Colonial Development." *Journal of the Royal African Society* 55: 22-56.

Rouche, Denise (1950) Les Villages de Libertie on A. O. F. *Bulletin de l'IFAN* 1: 135-215.

Salamone, Frank A. (1974) *Gods and Goods in Africa*. New Haven: HRAFlex.

————. (1977a) "The Methodological Significance of the Lying Informant." *Anthropological Quarterly* 50(5): 117-124.

————. (1977b) "Missionaries and Anthropologists: Competition or Reciprocity?" *Human Organization* 56 (Winter).

Savishinsky, Joel S. (1972) "Coping with Feuding: The Missionary, the Fur Trader, and the Ethnographer." *Human Organization* 81, 5: 281-90.

Schapera, Isaac. (1958) "Christianity and the Tswana." *Journal of the Royal Anthropological Institute* 8: 1-10.

Smith, M. G. (1969) "Some Developments in the Analytic Framework of Pluralism," pp. 415-58 in Leo Kuper and M.G. Smith (eds.) *Pluralism in Africa*. Berkeley: University of California Press.

Stone, Linda. (1997) *Kinship and Gender: An Introduction*. Boulder, CO: Westview Press.

Stavenhagen, Rodolfo. (1971) "Decolonizing Applied Social Sciences." *Human Organization* SO, 4: 854-48.

Tonkinson, Robert. (1974) *The Jigalong Mob*. Menlo Park, California: Cummings Publishing Company.

Van Baal, Jan. (1972) "Past Perfect," in Solon Kimball and James Watson (eds.) *Crossing Cultural Boundaries*. San Francisco: Chandler Publishing Company.

Van den Berghe, Pierre L. (1973) *Power and Privilege at an African University*. Cambridge.

Werthmann, Katja. "Matan bariki, 'Women of the Barracks'—Muslim Hausa women in an urban neighbourhood in Northern Nigeria." *Africa* 72.1 (2002): 112.

Index

About the Authors

Virginia A. Salamone is principal of Sacred Heart Elementary School in Hartsdale. She has taught college at the University of Jos, Nigeria, Elizabeth Seton College, Iona College, Mt. St. Vincent College, the College of New Rochelle, and Katherine Gibbs College. She has written and co-written a number of articles on Nigeria. Her major interests are education and the role of women in organizations. The idea of the Lucy Memorial Freed Slaves' Home book is hers, developed in Nigeria while working in the archives in Kaduna.

Frank A. Salamone is past Chair of Sociology and Anthropology at Iona College, New Rochelle, NY. He is married and he and his wife have two children. He has five other children, four living, nine grandchildren and a great-grandson. He has authored or edited more than 10 books, over 100 articles, numerous chapters, delivered many papers at national and international conferences, and is a member of many professional societies. He has conducted fieldwork in Nigeria, the United States, Venezuela and elsewhere.